Succulents
for Your
Home and Garden

A Guide to Growing 191 Beautiful Varieties & 11 Step-by-Step Crafts and Arrangements

T0322907

Gideon F. Smith and Jessica Surface

CRE**A**TIVE
HOMEOWNER®

CRE▲TIVE
HOMEOWNER®

Copyright © 2023 Jessica Surface, Gideon F. Smith, and Creative Homeowner

Succulents for Your Home and Garden (2023) contains content first published in *Cacti and Succulents Handbook, Expanded 2nd Edition* (2022), published by CompanionHouse Books, an imprint of Fox Chapel Publishing Company, Inc.

Succulents for Your Home and Garden
Managing Editor: Gretchen Bacon
Acquisitions Editor: Shelley Carr
Editor: Christa Oestreich
Designer: Wendy Reynolds
Proofreader: Kurt Conley
Indexer: Jay Kreider

Photographs by Jessica Surface: 3–6; 64–66; 82; 83 (chicken wire); 85 (top); 88–145.
Photographs by Gideon F. Smith: 9 (top left, bottom left, bottom right); 10–13; 14 (bottom right); 15–20; 21 (bottom); 22; 23 (left); 24; 25 (left, inset); 26–7; 28 (right); 29–41; 42 (right); 43–7; 48 (inset); 49–63; 148; 149 (left); 150–163; 164 (left); 165–9; 170 (right); 171–2; 173 (insets, left); 174–6; 177 (top left, top right); 178 (top right, left); 179–181; 182 (insets, top right, top bottom); 183–197; 198 (right); 199–212.
Contributor photos and captions are courtesy of their associated artist (unless otherwise stated), used with permission.
Shutterstock photos: vidimages (front cover, back cover, project opener, 1–5, 7, 59, 64–5, 80, 213, 216 succulent icons); kuroksta (8–58 hand icon); Irena Socratous (9 top right); Creative by Nature (14 top right); Rebekah Zemansky (14 left); Maren Winter (21 top); De19 (23 right); pjatnica (25 right); Jimenezar (28 left); panattar (42 left); Patrycja Nowak (48); rabarberts (80 scissors); nanantachoke (80 hot glue gun); maksimee (80 wire cutters); Florin Burlan, (80 gloves); worachet homkajon (81 screwdriver); Arsgera (81 staple gun); kasarp studio (81 drill); Seregam (81 measuring tape); Artem Stepanov (83 floral wire); Anton Starikov, (83 twine); Ekaterina43 (83 fishing line); igor kisselev (83 grapevine wire); Jenn Huls, (83 ribbon); allme (84 top right); Becky Starsmore (84 top left); Efetova (84 bottom left); Michelle Lee Photography (85 bottom); Deniza 40x (86–7); New Africa (146–47); Bilalstock (149 right); Kira Volkov (164 right); Natali Mali (170 left); Ladykhris (173 right); Sharaf Maksumov (177 bottom, 209 right); Alina Kuptsova (178 bottom right); TippyTortue, (182 top left); kampol Jongmeesuk (198 right).

ISBN 978-1-58011-572-8

Library of Congress Control Number: 2023936186

We are always looking for talented authors. To submit an idea, please send a brief inquiry to acquisitions@foxchapelpublishing.com.

Printed in China
First Printing

Creative Homeowner®, *www.creativehomeowner.com*, is an imprint of New Design Originals Corporation and distributed exclusively in North America by Fox Chapel Publishing Company, Inc., 800-457-9112, 903 Square Street, Mount Joy, PA 17552, and in the United Kingdom by Grantham Book Service, Trent Road, Grantham, Lincolnshire, NG31 7XQ.

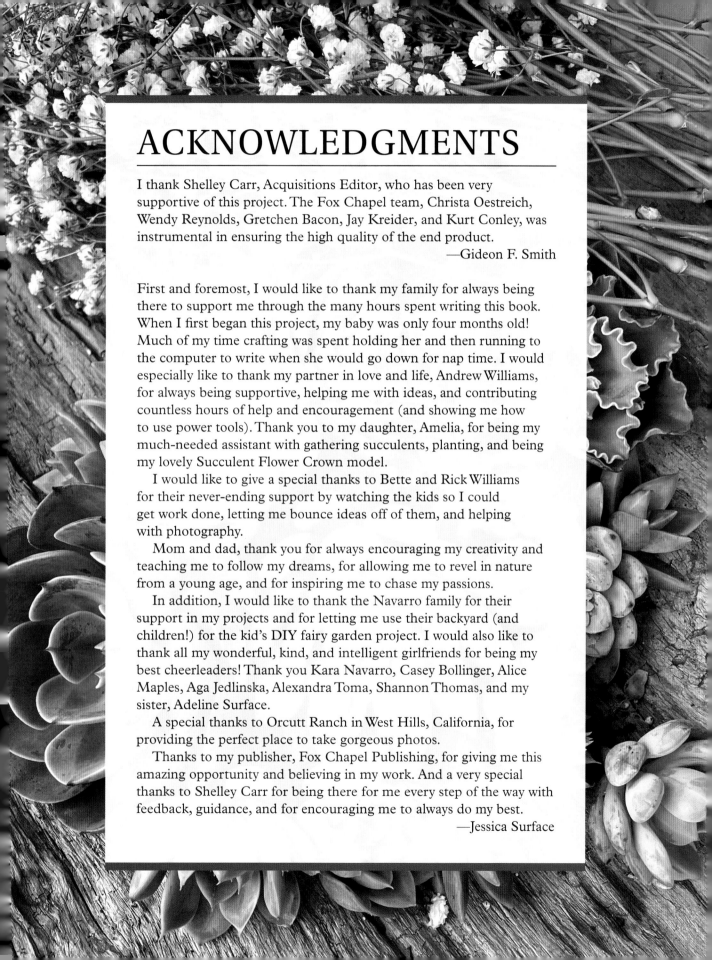

ACKNOWLEDGMENTS

I thank Shelley Carr, Acquisitions Editor, who has been very supportive of this project. The Fox Chapel team, Christa Oestreich, Wendy Reynolds, Gretchen Bacon, Jay Kreider, and Kurt Conley, was instrumental in ensuring the high quality of the end product.

—Gideon F. Smith

First and foremost, I would like to thank my family for always being there to support me through the many hours spent writing this book. When I first began this project, my baby was only four months old! Much of my time crafting was spent holding her and then running to the computer to write when she would go down for nap time. I would especially like to thank my partner in love and life, Andrew Williams, for always being supportive, helping me with ideas, and contributing countless hours of help and encouragement (and showing me how to use power tools). Thank you to my daughter, Amelia, for being my much-needed assistant with gathering succulents, planting, and being my lovely Succulent Flower Crown model.

I would like to give a special thanks to Bette and Rick Williams for their never-ending support by watching the kids so I could get work done, letting me bounce ideas off of them, and helping with photography.

Mom and dad, thank you for always encouraging my creativity and teaching me to follow my dreams, for allowing me to revel in nature from a young age, and for inspiring me to chase my passions.

In addition, I would like to thank the Navarro family for their support in my projects and for letting me use their backyard (and children!) for the kid's DIY fairy garden project. I would also like to thank all my wonderful, kind, and intelligent girlfriends for being my best cheerleaders! Thank you Kara Navarro, Casey Bollinger, Alice Maples, Aga Jedlinska, Alexandra Toma, Shannon Thomas, and my sister, Adeline Surface.

A special thanks to Orcutt Ranch in West Hills, California, for providing the perfect place to take gorgeous photos.

Thanks to my publisher, Fox Chapel Publishing, for giving me this amazing opportunity and believing in my work. And a very special thanks to Shelley Carr for being there for me every step of the way with feedback, guidance, and for encouraging me to always do my best.

—Jessica Surface

88

98

92

102

108

108

112

112

118

122

126

130

138

CONTENTS

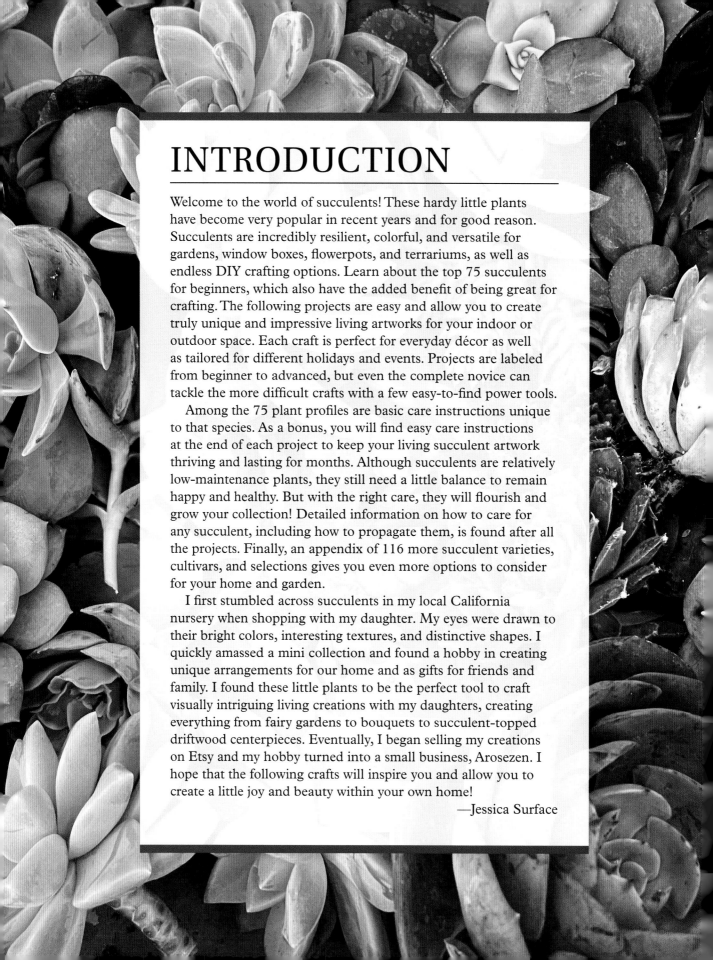

INTRODUCTION

Welcome to the world of succulents! These hardy little plants have become very popular in recent years and for good reason. Succulents are incredibly resilient, colorful, and versatile for gardens, window boxes, flowerpots, and terrariums, as well as endless DIY crafting options. Learn about the top 75 succulents for beginners, which also have the added benefit of being great for crafting. The following projects are easy and allow you to create truly unique and impressive living artworks for your indoor or outdoor space. Each craft is perfect for everyday décor as well as tailored for different holidays and events. Projects are labeled from beginner to advanced, but even the complete novice can tackle the more difficult crafts with a few easy-to-find power tools.

Among the 75 plant profiles are basic care instructions unique to that species. As a bonus, you will find easy care instructions at the end of each project to keep your living succulent artwork thriving and lasting for months. Although succulents are relatively low-maintenance plants, they still need a little balance to remain happy and healthy. But with the right care, they will flourish and grow your collection! Detailed information on how to care for any succulent, including how to propagate them, is found after all the projects. Finally, an appendix of 116 more succulent varieties, cultivars, and selections gives you even more options to consider for your home and garden.

I first stumbled across succulents in my local California nursery when shopping with my daughter. My eyes were drawn to their bright colors, interesting textures, and distinctive shapes. I quickly amassed a mini collection and found a hobby in creating unique arrangements for our home and as gifts for friends and family. I found these little plants to be the perfect tool to craft visually intriguing living creations with my daughters, creating everything from fairy gardens to bouquets to succulent-topped driftwood centerpieces. Eventually, I began selling my creations on Etsy and my hobby turned into a small business, Arosezen. I hope that the following crafts will inspire you and allow you to create a little joy and beauty within your own home!

—Jessica Surface

ABOUT SUCCULENTS

What separates a succulent from most plants is how water is stored in the leaves and stems. They are often fleshy, a consequence of the sap contained inside. This feature developed in a variety of ways, such as flowery rosettes, long strings, large ruffles, and small tree-like bunches. The wide variety of options rivals many flowers that are commonly found in the garden.

For anyone new to raising succulents or those new to crafting with them, here are profiles for the top 75 recommended varieties. Each profile will provide individual care instructions, but continue until the end of the section to learn even more about succulent care and propagation. What's great about these plants is that they require less care than many others. Whether you want something minimalistic or bursting with life, there is a succulent out there for you!

Top 75 Succulents For Crafting

AEONIUM

With about 35 species, the genus *Aeonium* is one of the smaller groups included in the family Crassulaceae. Their collective common name, tree houseleeks, is already an indication that most species develop short or even long stems atop of which tightly packed leaves are clustered into a rosulate arrangement. Many cultivars and hybrids exist that differ in size, shape, and color. These succulents are popular no matter which you choose.

Aeonium arboreum and Selections

Common name: Tree Aeonium

Size: 36" (1m), though some variants remain smaller

FEATURED SELECTIONS, CULTIVARS, AND HYBRIDS:
- *Aeonium arboreum* var. *arboreum*
- *Aeonium arboreum* var. *holochrysum*
- *Aeonium* 'Zwartkop' (common names: Black Rose and Zwartkop)
- *Aeonium* 'Atropurpureum' (common name: Atropurpureum)

Plants grow as medium-sized to large shrubs that have long, variously leaning stems and branches. With age, the lower leaves on the stems and branches are shed to expose fairly smooth, clean trunks that can reach a diameter of about 1" (2.5cm) in old specimens. The rather thin-succulent leaves are somewhat variable, but generally spatula-shaped in outline. Leaves are clustered into tight rosettes that are carried towards the tips of the branches. During the dry season—generally the warm to hot summer months—the leaf rosettes can be even more tightly arranged into golf ball–shaped clusters. Inflorescences are the shape of golden pyramids and densely packed with bright yellow flowers.

Several variants, mutations, and hybrids of *Aeonium arboreum* are in cultivation, with the best known of these being the cultivar *Aeonium* 'Zwartkop.' Its leaves are a uniform, deep black-purple color, and when planted en masse, present a spectacular color foil for companion succulents. In the cultivar *Aeonium* 'Atrpurpurea,' the purplish black color is often somewhat less intense and the centers of the leafy rosettes tend to be light green. The purple leaves can revert to being uniformly light green. In the case of *Aeonium arboretum* var. *holochrysum*, the leafy rosettes often remain smaller, upturned, very tightly clustered, and presented in the shape of small bowls at the tips of the clean stems and branches.

All these variants can be grown in containers, including indoors, but they really come into their own when planted in large drifts in open beds. If large, shrubby specimens—especially when plants start to age—are not required, cuttings of the upper inch or two of the branches can be taken and grown in pots or established outdoors in beds. The golden yellow inflorescences are spectacular, but not all the leafy rosettes will produce them in a season.

Aeonium arboreum var. *arboreum*

Aeonium arboreum var. *holochrysum*

Aeonium 'Zwartkop'

Aeonium 'Atropurpureum'

CARE INSTRUCTIONS

Plants thrive outdoors but should be given some protection where very low temperatures prevail. They will also grow well indoors or in a greenhouse.

Indoor care: Plants should be provided with sufficient light and the soil should be allowed to dry out between watering events.

Outdoor care: If grown outdoors, aeoniums generally prefer Mediterranean-type climates—cool, wet winters and hot, dry summers.

Temperature: Plants can tolerate quite low temperatures, and at around 32°F (0°C), virtually no damage is evident.

Lighting: Bright to filtered light.

Watering: Plants thrive on regular irrigation.

Repotting: Plants can be left in a container for several years, but will respond well to being repotted into fresh soil every two years, even if the same sized pot is used.

Propagating: Seed will germinate with great ease, which has given rise to the species becoming naturalized in several places well beyond its natural geographical distribution range on the Canary Islands. Stem cuttings and individual leaves also strike root with ease.

Aeonium haworthii

Common names: Mound Aeonium, Haworth's Aeonium, Pinwheel

Size: 12"–20" (30–50cm) tall

Plants grow as small shrubs that develop multiple stems from ground level. The stems are often rather thin and appear to be unable to support the leafy rosettes in an erect position. This gives rise to mound-shaped plants with rounded canopies. Leaf shape is variable, but leaves are generally spatula shaped. The leaves end in a sharp, but harmless, tip. Leaf margins are adorned with minute cilia and often red-rimmed. Whitish yellow to cream-colored flowers are carried in small, plump inflorescences that the stalks are too weak to keep flower clusters upright.

Aeonium haworthii is cultivated almost globally and easily adapts to local climatic and growing conditions. It has even become naturalized in some places, such as in Australia.

> *Aeonium* 'Kiwi' is a cultivar of *Aeonium haworthii*, meaning it is similar in appearance and care. 'Kiwi' is a favorite to use in succulent crafts.

CARE INSTRUCTIONS

Plants do well in containers that can be kept indoors or, preferably, outdoors.

Indoor care: Keep in bright light.

Outdoor care: Plants are very easy to grow in pots, where they look their best given their small size.

Temperature: Plants can tolerate low temperatures of even slightly below freezing without any ill effects.

Lighting: Dappled shade or full sun. Plants will also grow in deep shade, but then do not look their best.

Watering: Plants do well with regular irrigation but can also tolerate very dry conditions.

Repotting: Plants can be kept in the same soil in a small container for many years.

Propagating: Plants grow easily from stem cuttings.

Aeonium sedifolium

Common names: Dwarf Aeonium, Pixie Aeonium

Size: 5"–8" (12–20cm) tall

Plants grow as miniature shrublets that develop numerous stems, carrying clusters of small, spatula-shaped leaves toward the branch apices. The stems are thin, variously twisted, and bent under the weight of the leaf clusters. The bright, light green leaves of the species can be sticky—sand and soil will stick to the leaves—and are variously adorned with scattered, red, mostly longitudinal, sections. Inflorescences consist of numerous yellow flowers.

The species does best in winter-rainfall regions, but will also grow in places that receive summer rainfall, where flowering is sometimes impaired. Plants can be best displayed when grown in small or even miniature containers. The red leaf maculation contributes to the attraction of the plants. Like most aeoniums, plants will easily hybridize with a range of other species of this genus, and many plants sold under the name *Aeonium sedifolia* are actually hybrids.

CARE INSTRUCTIONS
Plants grow well outdoors, especially when kept in small containers. The pots can also be kept indoors.
Indoor care: Keep plants in a sunny spot.
Outdoor care: If grown in a container, plants can be moved under cover in summer-rainfall areas because plants will be in their resting phase.
Temperature: Plants will be damaged or even killed outright at temperatures below 32°F (0°C).
Lighting: Full sun.
Watering: Plants are very drought tolerant, but benefit from irrigation during the winter season when they actively grow. In the hot summer months, plants are dormant and don't need to be watered regularly.
Repotting: Plants can be kept in the same soil in a container for several years.
Propagating: Grow from stem cuttings.

This bowl of succulents is used as an outdoor table decoration. A small clump of the yellow-flowered *Aeonium sedifolium* grows in the center of the container.

Aeonium tabuliforme

Common names: Saucer Plant, Flat-Topped Aeonium

Size: 1"–2" (2.5–5cm) tall, 8" (20cm) wide

The rosettes grow flat on the ground and remain saucer-like until they flower. The rosettes are produced on short, unbranched stems that are completely hidden. The rosettes themselves consist of a multitude of somewhat fleshy, bright green leaves. The leaves are tightly packed—almost like fish scales—and have fine cilia along their margins. After three to four years of vegetative growth, plants will develop inflorescences that can be over 24" (60cm) tall. An inflorescence consists of numerous, small, yellowish white flowers.

CARE INSTRUCTIONS
Plants will grow well outdoors or indoors in a container.
Indoor care: Keep in a dappled-shady spot.
Outdoor care: Plants are well adapted to grow on vertical surfaces where water will not collect and remain on the flat rosettes. Plants usually die after having flowered, but are well worth growing for their fascinating rosette shape.
Temperature: Plants will be damaged below 32°F (0°C).
Lighting: Plants grow well in dappled shade.
Watering: Plants benefit from regular irrigation.
Repotting: Should ideally be planted in a container that is large enough to allow it to reach flowering maturity without requiring repotting.
Propagating: Individual leaves that are carefully removed from the stem will strike root. Offsets, which are not produced in abundance, from the main rosette can also be grown on.

ASTERACEAE

This plant family, also known as the "Daisy family," covers a large range of flowering plants—most of which aren't succulents. However, the succulents found here are prized both for their leaves and flowers, making a perfect potted plant.

×*Bacurio delphinatifolius*

Common names: String of Dolphins, Jumping Dolphins

Stem size: 12"–20" (30–50cm) long

Plants are thin stemmed with small, succulent leaves widely dispersed along the stems. Leaves of ×*Bacurio delphinatifolius* show some variation, but usually consist of a prominently projecting, windowed central portion and two shorter, lateral lobes with parts of the incised blade variously recurved, so resembling miniature dolphins. The tiny, white flowers are tightly packed in small, head-shaped inflorescences.

The name ×*Bacurio delphinatifolius* was published for the hybrid between *Baculellum articulatum*

(previously often treated as *Curio articulatus*) and *Curio rowleyanus*. The shape of the leaves has given rise to the hybrid being known under the trade designations 'String of Dolphins' and 'Jumping Dolphins.'

CARE INSTRUCTIONS

Plants do well both indoors and outdoors.
Indoor care: Grow the plants in a pot or in a hanging basket in a brightly lit place.
Outdoor care: Plants should be placed in a sunny spot or in dappled shade.
Temperature: Plants are not cold hardy below 32°F (0°C).
Lighting: Plants look their best in bright light. In low light conditions, the stem segments between the leaves can elongate unnaturally.
Watering: Plants benefit from a weekly drenching. Make sure the soil is well drained. If plants are kept in small pots in a very arid region, water more frequently.
Repotting: Plants can remain in the same soil for several years. The stems grow rapidly and will soon dangle waterfall-like over the edge of a container. This makes it a perfect plant to grow in a hanging basket.
Propagating: Stem cuttings can be placed on the soil surface, covered with a thin layer of soil, and soon the cuttings will sprout roots.

Curio crassulifolius

Common names: Blue Chalksticks, Blue Fingers

Size: 12"–20" (30–50cm) tall

The evergreen, perennial plants grow upright, leaning, or sprawling. The stems are smooth and lack hairs. Leaves are cylindrical, 1"–2" (2.5–5cm) long, grayish blue to light green, and terminate in a pointed tip. The leaves, which are covered in a light, waxy bloom, are carried in dense clusters toward the branch tips. The small, head-shaped inflorescences—technically called capitula—are small, and generally only a few are carried on slender, branched inflorescence stalks. The tiny, densely packed flowers are white to creamy or sometimes yellowish.

Curio crassulifolius is a carpet-forming, waterwise succulent that will rapidly cover a small or large denuded area if planted 9" (20cm) apart. Plants do very well in any soil type, including in coastal gardens with very sandy soil and in clay soil. Curio crassulifolius is sometimes known as Kleinia crassulifolius.

CARE INSTRUCTIONS

If kept indoors in pots, even in brightly lit positions, plants will lose much of their charm. This is really a plant that should be grown outdoors.

Outdoor care: Plants are remarkably undemanding in cultivation. When planted en masse, blocks of blue foliage can be created; when planted in strips, they will establish as near-blue sections in a bed. Plants grow well in virtually any position that receives full sun, including in rockeries.

Temperature: Short spells of temperatures around 32°F (0°C) can be tolerated, but heavy frosts will kill the plants.

Lighting: Grow Curio crassulifolius in a position that receives full sun. Even in semi-shade, plants can become unnaturally etiolated with the branches becoming floppy.

Watering: Very little irrigation is needed. The soil should ideally be well drained, but plants can also grow in clay soils. However, the better the drainage, the less the chances that plants will succumb to root rot.

Repotting: Plants can be grown in pots for many years without repotting being necessary. Rather, when refreshed material is needed, take stem cuttings and plant them in pots filled with fresh soil that is well drained.

Propagating: Stem cuttings of about 2"–3" (5–7cm) long, taken from young or old growth, will develop roots within a few weeks if placed in a well-drained (but moist) rooting medium.

The blue-leaved Curio crassulifolius contrasts sharply with the light green, red-margined leaves of Kalanchoe ×estrelae.

Curio radicans

Common names: String of Bananas, String of Fishhooks

Stem size: 12"–24" (30–60cm) long

Plants produce long, creeping or dangling stems that are too weak to remain upright. The stems carry small, banana-shaped leaves short distances apart. In some variants, the leaves are shiny green when grown in the shade or can turn a coppery brown color when under water stress. The tiny, white flowers are borne in small head-shaped inflorescences.

This species is grown for the shape and size of its leaves, rather than for its small white flowers. Leaf shape can vary somewhat, as with the variant with prominently hook-shaped leaves commonly known as 'String-of-Fishhooks.' *Curio radicans* is sometimes known as *Kleinia radicans* or as *Senecio radicans*.

CARE INSTRUCTIONS

Plants grow well both indoors and outdoors.
Indoor care: This is a perfect plant to keep indoors in a pot or a hanging basket in a brightly lit position. The leaves are plump and shiny light green when well grown.
Outdoor care: In mild climates, plants can be grown outdoors in beds as a groundcover, or in rockeries where their stems will dangle over rocks.
Temperature: Plants can tolerate temperatures of around 32°F (0°C) for short spells, but are not frost resistant for long periods. However, they are more cold tolerant than most other succulent daisies.
Lighting: Full sun or dappled shade.

Watering: Plants are very drought tolerant, and irrigation is only required once the soil has dried out. If plants are kept too dry, the leaves tend to develop a longitudinal furrow. This is a good indication that plants should be watered more regularly.
Repotting: Plants can be kept in the same soil for many years. Repot them into fresh soil after about three years.
Propagating: Any length of stem can be removed with a pair of pruning shears, placed on the soil surface, and covered with a thin layer of soil. Roots will soon develop.

Curio rowleyanus

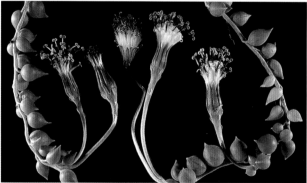

Common names: String of Pearls, String of Beads

Stem size: 36" (1m) long

Plants produce long, thin stems that creep along the ground or dangle over other plants, rocks, or rims of pots. Leaves resemble peas, with each leaf sporting a small tip and a narrow, longitudinal, opaque window. The flowers are small, white, and densely clustered into head-shaped inflorescences. The stamens that protrude above the flowers are purple and the pollen yellow, which gives the otherwise drab flowers a semblance of color.

Curio rowleyanus, like *C. radicans*, is a perfect plant for growing in a hanging basket or in a small pot. The stems will dangle curtain-like over the rim of the pot. An attractive variegated form of the species is available in the trade. In this mutation, the leaves have large creamy white sections. *Curio rowleyanus* is sometimes known as *Kleinia rowleyana* or as *Senecio rowleyanus*.

CARE INSTRUCTIONS

Plants grow very well both indoors and outdoors.

Indoor care: Plants will do well in pots or hanging baskets in brightly lit areas but can also tolerate some shade. However, too much shade will result in the stems becoming etiolated.

Outdoor care: Plants will grow well outdoors in mild climates, preferably in pots or hanging baskets. To look their best, plants require little more than regular watering and bright light.

Temperature: Plants will survive temperatures slightly below 32°F (0°C) for short periods, but prolonged exposure to such conditions will eventually kill the plants.

Lighting: Plants prefer bright light.

Watering: Plants benefit from regular watering—about once a week. If water is withheld for extended periods, the pea-shaped leaves will become shriveled.

Repotting: Plants can be kept in the same soil for a few years. Repot into fresh soil after two years. Use the same-sized pot.

Propagating: Plants can be easily propagated from stem cuttings. Remove a piece of stem and place it on the soil surface. Cover with a thin layer of soil. Roots will soon develop. If the stems segment is very long, simply roll it up and place it on the soil before covering it with a thin layer of soil.

Kleinia petraea

Common names: Creeping Jade, Trailing Jade

Size: 4"–5" (10–13cm) tall

Stem size: 12"–15" (30–38cm) long

The light green, elongated-coin-shaped leaves are flat and thick, taking on a purple-brown color in winter. Leaves overlap like roof tiles along the stems. The leaves resemble those of *Crassula ovata*, which is commonly known as the jade plant, hence the common name of *Kleinia petraea* (creeping jade). The elongated, head-shaped inflorescences carry numerous tightly packed, orange flowers.

This creeping or trailing plant has become very popular in cultivation as it can serve multiple purposes in the garden. It grows well in hanging baskets from which the leafy stems will dangle down. Alternatively, it can be used as a groundcover as the fleshy but weak stems root as they "creep" across the ground. When temperatures drop and plants remain dry, the leaves of *Kleinia petraea* take on a purple-brown hue. *Kleinia petraea* is often still known as *Senecio jacobsenii*.

CARE INSTRUCTIONS

Plants are best grown outdoors, but will also grow in pots kept indoors. Leaves of plants kept outdoors are often strongly pinkish orange to purple-brown-infused, while the leaves of plants kept indoors tend to remain uniformly light green.

Indoor care: Keep plants in a brightly lit place.

Outdoor care: Plants grow very well in open beds and in pots. Plants should be established in sunny positions or in dappled shade.

Temperature: Plants are not cold hardy and exposure to 32°F (0°C), even for short spells, will kill the plants.

Lighting: Plants grow best in bright light.

Watering: Plants are very drought tolerant and should only be watered once the soil in which they are grown has dried out.

Repotting: Plants will grow well in containers for many years without repotting being required. Once the soil needs to be refreshed, plants can be reestablished in the same-sized pot.

Propagating: Plants can be propagated from stem cuttings.

Othonna capensis

Common names: Ruby Necklace, Baby Toes, Little Pickles, Cape Aster

Stem size: 12"–24" (30–60cm) tall

Plants are low-growing and develop numerous, thin stems that creep along the ground or will scramble into and over plants with which they grow. The usually densely leaved, trailing stems will soon dangle down under the weight of the foliage. Small, jelly bean–shaped leaves with pointed tips are carried at short intervals along the stems. The stems and leaves can become red-infused in strong sunlight. Fairly large, yellow-flowered inflorescences are borne on long stalks.

Unlike the drab-colored flowers of *Curio radicans* and *Curio rowleyanus*, those of *Othonna capensis* are bright yellow. What looks like yellow petals are in fact small ray florets. *Othonna capensis* is sometimes known as *Crassothonna capensis*.

CARE INSTRUCTIONS

Plants can be grown indoors or outdoors.

Indoor care: Plants take on a characteristic reddish sheen when kept in bright light. In shade, the stems can become etiolated.

Outdoor care: Plants grow best in full sun, but can also be kept in dappled shade.

Temperature: Plants are not frost hardy and anything more than very brief exposure to 32°F (0°C) will kill the plants outright.

Lighting: Bright light conditions are required to bring out the best colors of the foliage and stems.

Watering: Plants benefit from regular watering—about once a week—to prevent the leaves from shriveling.

Repotting: Plants can be kept in the same pot for many years before tipping the plants out and refreshing the soil.

Propagating: Plants can be easily grown from stem cuttings.

CRASSULA

It is mostly the extensive range of leaf shapes, sizes, and colors found in *Crassula*, one of the largest genera in the family Crassulaceae, that makes them such popular plants to grow. Every succulent here brings unique characteristics that are sure to make them shine on their own and stand apart from other species.

Crassula arborescens subsp. *arborescens*

Common names: Silver Dollar Plant, Silver Jade Plant

Size: 36" (1m) tall

In open beds, plants can grow as medium to large shrubs. However, stem cuttings of only 2"–3" (5–8cm) long will easily strike root, and when root-run is limited in a small container, the cuttings will happily grow as bonsai-ed specimens for many years.

Their multistemmed clusters form haphazardly rounded canopies. Stems remain upright but could in time topple over under the weight of the leaf clusters. Leaves are spoon-shaped and range from nearly white to a ghostly silver color, hence the common name. Leaves could have a red margin and conspicuous red dots on both the upper and lower surfaces, adding to the charm of the species. The star-shaped flowers are generally bright white and arranged in round clusters.

Plants could be shy to flower, especially if they are still young and the roots are pot bound. However, in the open ground, plants will flower profusely, with the snowball-shaped and -colored flower clusters often covering the entire plant.

CARE INSTRUCTIONS

Plants will thrive outdoors in mild climates and grow well indoors, where its size will be limited by the size of the container in which it is grown.

Indoor care: Keep in a brightly lit spot, for example on a windowsill.

Outdoor care: Plants grow very well outdoors in virtually any soil type.

Temperature: Plants do not do well in very low temperatures. If exposed to 32°F (0°C) or lower temperatures for prolonged periods, serious frost damage will be evident.

Lighting: Bright to filtered light.

Watering: Allow the soil to dry out between watering events.

Repotting: Plants can remain in pots, even small ones, for many years. When repotting, use a pot one size bigger than the one from which the plants are tipped out.

Propagating: Plants can be propagated from stem cuttings or individual leaves. Place leaves on top of—not in—the soil.

Crassula arborescens subsp. *undulatifolia*

Common names: Ripple Jade, Undulata

Size: Under 36" (1m) tall

Plants grow as small to medium shrubs that develop densely branched, mound-like canopies. Plants therefore tend to spread horizontally as well as vertically. The thin-succulent leaves are distinctly wavy, bluish-white, and often red-margined. Flowers, borne in small, rounded clusters, are white and star-shaped.

Plants tend to be weakly deciduous—more so than *C. arborescens* subsp. *arborescens*—and naturally shed some of their leaves in very dry and cold conditions. It also has a smaller stature than its cousin, *C. arborescens* subsp. *arborescens*.

CARE INSTRUCTIONS

Plants will thrive outdoors in mild climates and grow well indoors, where its size will be limited by the size of the container in which it is grown.

Indoor care: Plants are not difficult to keep indoors if attention is paid to regular watering—do not let plants become completely dehydrated—and pots are placed in well-lit areas.

Outdoor care: Plants will thrive in full sun or in dappled shade in mild climates.

Temperature: If exposed to 32°F (0°C) or lower temperatures for prolonged periods, serious frost damage will be evident. Plants are slightly more frost-hardy than *C. arborescens* subsp. *arborescens*.

Lighting: Bright light.

Watering: The soil should be allowed to dry out between watering events, but since the leaves are generally only thin-succulent, plants ideally should not be left without irrigation for extended periods.

Repotting: Plants will remain small when grown in containers that allow only limited root growth.

Propagating: Plants are easy to propagate from stem cuttings and even shoot tips. Leaves, if placed on top of the soil, will also develop roots and eventually new plants.

Crassula capitella subsp. *capitella* 'Campfire Plant'

Common names: Campfire Crassula, Firecracker

Size: 12" (30cm) tall

Plants branch from the base to form small clusters. Branches grow upright at first but can later become leaning. The often strongly orange-red leaves are arranged in four-ranked rosettes. Leaves are elongated-triangular to sword-shaped and smooth, except sometimes with short, stiff hairs along the margins. Long, tapering inflorescences with small, white flowers are produced from summer through autumn.

Crassula capitella subsp. *capitella* 'Campfire Plant' is a superb groundcover. When established about 6" (15cm) apart, they will quickly cover a denuded area.

CARE INSTRUCTIONS

Plants are perfect for growing outdoors and will also thrive indoors.
Indoor care: Keep in very bright light and water sparingly.
Outdoor care: Plant in full sun to ensure that the leaves retain the orange-red coloration.
Temperature: Plants are frost tender.
Lighting: Full sun.
Watering: Plants can survive with minimal irrigation.
Repotting: Renew plants annually by taking cuttings and establishing them in fresh soil.
Propagating: Plants grow easily from stem cuttings.

Crassula ericoides subsp. *ericoides*

Common name: Miniature Fir Tree Crassula, Pipe Cleaner Crassula

Size: 12" (30cm) tall

With the lower portions of stems and branches being devoid of leaves, the growth form of the plants is reminiscent to that of small fir trees. When a number of them are clustered together in bonsai pots, they will form a striking, miniature landscape. The bright green leaves are very short, shaped like pine needles, and borne only along the upper parts of the stems and branches. Leaves are arranged in four ranks, giving the upper parts of the stems a feathery appearance. During late summer and early winter, small yellow-white flowers are borne on very short stalks at the branch tips.

CARE INSTRUCTIONS

Plants will grow well indoors and outdoors.
Indoor care: Keep in bright light.
Outdoor care: Plants will grow well in full sun and in dappled shade.
Temperature: Plants are frost tender.
Lighting: Bright light.
Watering: Plants are very drought hardy. The soil in which they are grown only needs a good drenching once it has dried out.
Repotting: Plants will grow in small containers for many years without losing their vitality or visual attraction.
Propagating: Plants can be grown from stem and branch cuttings. Very short, leafy branch tips will also strike root with ease.

Crassula multicava

Common names: Fairy Crassula, London's Pride

Size: 12"–24" (30–60cm) tall

Plants grow as small to medium shrublets that will quickly develop several stems and branches that tend to become leaning, rooting where they touch the soil. The greenish stems are soft, succulent, and like all plant parts, smooth; stems can be infused with pink. Leaves are bright shiny green, round in outline, and carried on short stalks. Small pinkish white flowers are carried sparsely in many-branched inflorescences. Especially post-flowering, small plantlets develop on the inflorescences.

Stems are brittle, and any that break off will root where they fall. *Crassula multicava* is a very useful, rapid-growing groundcover.

CARE INSTRUCTIONS

Plants will thrive both indoors and outdoors.
Indoor care: When kept indoors, plants will grow well even in rather low light conditions.
Outdoor care: Plants grow best in semi-shade, and will also do well in deep shade.
Temperature: Although plants are not frost hardy for extended periods, they will survive low temperatures for short spells.
Lighting: Plants thrive in semi-shade and will even grow in deep shade.
Watering: Plants prefer soil that is kept moist.
Repotting: Repotting can be delayed for several years. Rather, after having flowered, plants can be trimmed right down, after which new branches will sprout from the base.
Propagating: Plants regenerate with ease from the plantlets that develop on the inflorescences. Stem cuttings will also root easily.

Crassula ovata

Common names: Jade Plant, Money Plant

Size: 48" (1.2m) tall

Plants grow as small to robust shrubs in open beds; however, small branches can be placed in pots and will remain stunted, but perfectly healthy, for many years. With age, the stems and branches will take on a rough appearance. The leaves are coin-shaped—oval to round in outline—from which the common name, money plant, is derived. The small flowers range from white to pink and are carried in ball-shaped clusters.

The jade plant has been a popular indoor plant in Europe for several centuries. A bewildering range of strikingly beautiful variants of the species have been selected for the horticultural trade (see page 22).

CARE INSTRUCTIONS

Plants do equally well indoors and outdoors.
Indoor care: Plants are not particular about their growing conditions and will easily grow in bright light, but will also thrive in low light conditions.
Outdoor care: Plants will grow in full sun, in dappled shade, or even in deep shade.
Temperature: Plants will survive short spells of subzero temperatures. However, in such conditions, leaves and the upper portions of stems can be expected to die back.
Lighting: Bright to low light conditions.
Watering: Water only once the soil has dried out.
Repotting: Plants can be left in their containers for many years. If a stunted specimen is required, replace the soil and replant the specimen into the same-sized container.
Propagating: Plants are very easy to grow from stem cuttings, which will root without any trouble. Leaves placed on top of the soil will also develop new plantlets at their base.

Crassula ovata Selections

Size: 12"–24" (30–60cm) tall

FEATURED SELECTIONS:

- Gollum Jade Plant
- Baby Jade
- Dwarf Jade Plant
- Hummel's Sunset
- Lady Fingers
- Minima

A large range of selections of *C. ovata* have become very popular in both indoor and outdoor domestic horticulture. Plants generally remain smaller growing than the regular form of the species. Variation, especially in terms of plant size and leaf shape and color, has been the driving force behind making these selections available. Leaf shape varies from narrowly cylindrical to nearly tubular, from egg-shaped to round, and variously folded. Several of the selections have white- or yellow-variegated leaves, colors that become enhanced in full sun. Flowers range in color from white to strongly pink-infused and are borne in small ball-shaped clusters.

To enhance the colors of the variegated-leaved selections, bright light is required. Withholding water also contributes to the leaves being more intensely colored. If plants are kept too dry for prolonged periods, whole branches will be shed.

CARE INSTRUCTIONS

Plants do well both indoors and outdoors in mild climates. In more severe climates, plants should be kept indoors.

Indoor care: To retain their attraction, these selections generally require bright light conditions.

Outdoor care: Full sun.

Temperature: Plants are not cold hardy and will not tolerate subfreezing temperatures.

Lighting: Bright light.

Watering: Water only once the soil has dried out.

Repotting: Plants need not be repotted often. Especially if stunted specimens are desired, repotting should be delayed.

Propagating: Plants can be easily propagated from stem cuttings, and in most cases, also from leaves that are left on the soil surface.

Crassula ovata 'Baby Jade'

Crassula ovata 'Hummel's Sunset'

Crassula ovata 'Lady Fingers'

A selection of *Crassula ovata* that is sold under various monikers, such as 'Hummel's Sunset' or 'Tricolor.' Here, the striking bright golden yellow color of the crassula contrasts with the scarlet red flowers of *Echeveria affinis*.

Crassula pellucida subsp. marginalis

Common names: Calico Kitten, Trailing Crassula, Red Margin

Stem size: 12" (30cm) long

Plants develop numerous thin, weak stems that do not remain upright. Rather, they become creeping or trailing and will spill over the edge of a pot. The leaves are arranged along the purplish stem at short intervals. The opposite leaves in a pair are basally fused, or nearly so, which gives the impression that the leaf blades are continuous and that the stem is threaded through them. The light green leaves are heart-shaped to triangular in outline and often have a very pronounced red margin. Flowers are small, white to pale pink, and borne in few-flowered clusters.

The red leaf margins become much more pronounced in bright sunlight. In shaded positions, plants still grow well, but are not as chromatic.

CARE INSTRUCTIONS

Plants will grow well indoors in pots or in hanging baskets, as well as outside, in open beds, pots, or hanging baskets.

Indoor care: Plants will grow well indoors if kept in a bright position. Plants lose some of their charm if light levels are too low.

Outdoor care: Plants perform very well in rock gardens, where their thin, leafy stems will dangle over rocks and retaining walls. It is also a quick-growing groundcover and will rapidly fill up a pot and hanging basket, with the stems trailing over the rim.

Temperature: Plants are not cold hardy and show frost damage at 32°F (0°C).

Lighting: Plants grow well in bright sunlight as well as in dappled and even deep shade.

Watering: Plants are drought hardy and the soil in which they are cultivated should be allowed to dry out before watering.

Repotting: Place stem cuttings of a few inches long on top of the soil and sift a very thin layer of soil over them. Roots will soon develop.

Propagating: Plants are easy from stem cuttings, or simply divide up a clump and place the roots and stems into fresh soil.

Crassula perforata subsp. perforata

Common names: String of Buttons, Kebab Plant, Sosatie Bush

Size: 12"–16" (30–40cm) tall

Plants produce numerous thin, scraggly but leafy stems from the base. The stems generally do not branch. The blue-green, often red-margined, oppositely arranged, egg-shaped leaves are basally fused around the stem. This gives the impression of a series of evenly spaced buttons strung together. If plants are grown in a container, the stems will in time cascade over the rim to create a waterfall effect. During the summer very small, creamy white flowers are produced on thin inflorescences that extend from the stem tips.

CARE INSTRUCTIONS
Plants do well both indoors and outdoors in mild climates.

Indoor care: Plants will grow well indoors if given sufficient light.

Outdoor care: When planted outdoors, plants will grow into densely branched, horizontally spreading, shrub-like bushes. Plants do best in dappled-shady or fully exposed positions.

Temperature: Plants are not cold hardy and heavy frosts will kill them.

Lighting: Bright light.

Watering: Allow the soil to dry out between watering events.

Repotting: Plants generally benefit from being repotted every two years.

Propagating: Plants can be grown from stem cuttings.

Crassula rubricaulis

Common name: Red-Stemmed Crassula

Size: 8"–12" (20–30cm) tall

Plants develop into small, densely branched shrublets. The stems and branches are reddish, while the egg-shaped leaves can also be strongly red infused. The leaf margins are usually adorned with very fine cilia-like hairs. Small, white flowers are carried in clusters toward the branch tips. Plants make useful groundcovers because the shrublets also tend to spread horizontally.

CARE INSTRUCTIONS
Plants thrive outdoors in mild climates as well as indoors.

Indoor care: Keep plants in a place that receives bright light.

Outdoor care: Plants flourish when planted in full sun.

Temperature: Plants are not cold hardy and heavy frosts will kill them.

Lighting: Bright light.

Watering: Allow the soil to dry out between irrigation events.

Repotting: Plants benefit from biennial repotting into fresh soil.

Propagating: Plants can be grown from stem and branch cuttings that will easily root.

Crassula rupestris

Common names: Baby Necklace, Buttons on a String, Kebab Bush

Size: 12" (30cm) tall

Plants grow as small to medium, many-branched shrubs that often occur wedged between rocks in the native habitat of the species. Especially lower down, the stems and branches take on a woody character, while they are soft and more herbaceous higher up. The oppositely arranged leaves are triangular in outline and usually a light green to blue-green color. However, especially when under environmental stress, the leaves turn yellowish; in some variants the margins of the leaves can turn bright red. Small, white to light pink to more intensely pink flowers are carried in rounded clusters toward the branch tips.

CARE INSTRUCTIONS

Plants do very well when grown outdoors but can also be kept indoors in pots.

Indoor care: Keep plants in bright light.

Outdoor care: Plants grow well in a range of soil types as long the soil is well drained.

Temperature: Plants are not cold hardy and show frost damage at 32°F (0°C).

Lighting: Plants do best in strong sunlight.

Watering: Plants need only be watered once the soil in which they grow is dry.

Repotting: Plants can remain in the same soil in a pot for several years. Repot once plants appear pot bound.

Propagating: Cuttings of about 4" (10cm) long should be taken at the end of the resting period.

After allowing the cut end to seal, place in a well-drained mixture, for example gritty sand, which should be kept moist (not drenched).

Crassula sarcocaulis subsp. sarcocaulis

Common names: Miniature Baobab, Bonsai Crassula

Size: Under 36" (1m) tall

Plants are many-branched shrubs with smooth, thick, grayish brown stems and branches. Leaves are small and shield-shaped, and only thin-succulent. As winter approaches, the leaves are shed, which exposes the attractive stems and branches. Flowers are small and loosely packed in inflorescences that develop at the tips of the branches. Flower color ranges from white to pinkish red.

When plants dry out, even whole branch segments—typically the terminal 1"–2" (2.5–5cm)—will be shed. These branch pieces will very easily root where they fall. The canopies of this shrub can be pruned if they become too dense.

CARE INSTRUCTIONS

Plants do equally well indoors and outdoors.

Indoor care: Keep in bright light conditions and water regularly to keep the soil moist.

Outdoor care: Plants thrive in full sun and in semi-shade, but will also grow in low-light conditions.

Temperature: Some forms of the species are remarkably cold tolerant and will easily survive in subzero temperatures.

Lighting: Bright light.

Watering: Although plants will easily survive very dry conditions, they will somewhat surprisingly tolerate very wet conditions. In their natural habitats, they often grow in hollowed-out rock pans that will be inundated for days, even weeks, after a downpour.

Repotting: Plants can be kept in the same container for many years.

Propagating: Plants are easy to grow from stem cuttings of virtually any length.

Crassula sarmentosa var. sarmentosa

Common names: Trailing Jade, Comet, Variegata

Size: 20" (50cm) tall

Plants produce numerous, soft, densely light green–dotted stems that will trail down an embankment or creep along the ground. Pairs of somewhat arrowhead-shaped, dark green leaves are carried

sparsely along the stems and branches. Leaf margins are finely sawtooth-like serrated. Plants are quick-growing and as a groundcover will quickly cover a denuded area. Flowers are bright white and loosely packed in short, branched inflorescences.

Variegated-leaved variants of the species are available in the trade with several names, such as 'Comet' and 'Variegata,' applied to them. The variegation can be light yellow, golden yellow, or white. Given the trailing habit of the plants, they make very good subjects for cultivating in hanging baskets.

CARE INSTRUCTIONS

Plants thrive both indoors and outdoors.

Indoor care: A very versatile plant that will grow well indoors in brightly lit or shaded positions.

Outdoor care: Plants grow well in full sun, but will also thrive in dappled or full shade.

Temperature: Plants are not cold hardy.

Lighting: Bright light, semi-shade, or even deep shade.

Watering: Plants thrive on regular irrigation. The soil should ideally not dry out completely.

Repotting: Plants do not need regular repotting, but pruning the plants will yield more compact growth.

Propagating: Plants grow very easily from stem cuttings that will rapidly root where they are left on the soil.

Crassula tetragona subsp. *tetragona*

Common name: Miniature Pine Tree

Size: 24" (60cm) tall

Plants grow as sparse- to many-branched shrublets that carry their stems and branches upright. The stems and branches are densely or sparsely covered in short, pointed leaves that can be pointed upward or project horizontally sideways. Leaves are dull to light green, and usually arranged in four vertical ranks to give the plants a very tidy and symmetrical appearance. The white flowers are very small and carried in sparse inflorescences.

With their short, pointed leaves, plants look very much like pine tree seedlings—hence the common name. If planted closely together in a bonsai pot as a small cluster of short stems, plants make a striking composition. Plants will remain low growing for a very long time.

CARE INSTRUCTIONS

Plants grow well both indoors and outdoors.
Indoor care: Plants grow well in containers kept indoors, especially if placed in a sunny spot.
Outdoor care: Plants will easily grow in a range of soil types and are very undemanding in cultivation.
Temperature: Plants should not be exposed to subzero temperatures for extended periods.
Lighting: Plants do best where they receive bright light.
Watering: Plants are very drought-hardy and need only be watered once the soil has dried out completely.
Repotting: Repotting need only be done at very long intervals. Even root-bound specimens will remain healthy and look very natural.
Propagating: Plants grow easily from stem cuttings of any length.

VARIOUS CRASSULACEAE

All the succulents in this section are included in the family Crassulaceae. Here they are grouped in smaller categories—genera or hybrid genera (also referred to as nothogenera)—to point out their unique characteristics. These are a sampling of various Crassulaceae that are must-haves for their range of classic shapes and colors.

Graptopetalum paraguayense

Common names: Ghost Plant, Pink Ghost

Size: 3"–10" (7.5–25cm) tall, 2" (5cm) wide

Plants grow as small clusters of numerous stems that initially remain upright but soon become drooping. Stems are usually devoid of leaves lower down, with the leaves clustered into tight rosettes toward the tips of the stems. The color of the spatula-shaped leaves varies from light blue-green to nearly white, and can be light orange- or pink-infused. Inflorescences carry the white, star-shaped flowers in sparse clusters. The white petals are adorned with small, red flecks.

Very little care is required once plants have become established. This is a succulent that will grow very well in hanging baskets.

CARE INSTRUCTIONS
Plants can be grown indoors or outdoors.
Indoor care: Keep plants in well-lit places.
Outdoor care: Plants look their best if exposed to full sun.
Temperature: Plants are cold hardy to 20°F (-7°C).

Lighting: Plants should be given bright light; can be grown in dappled shade or, ideally, in full sun.
Watering: Being drought tolerant, plants only need to be watered once the soil in which they grow has dried out.
Repotting: Plants can be kept in the same soil for a long time. Leaves easily become detached from a stem and it is easier to establish stem cuttings in fresh soil than to repot a specimen.
Propagating: Plants grow easily from stem cuttings and from individual leaves placed on the soil surface. The leaves will quickly develop roots and new plants from the base.

Graptopetalum paraguayense is a popular option for planting as well as for succulent crafts. Because of this, there are a great deal of cultivars, hybrids, and selections that are similar in appearance and care, such asx *Graptopetalum* 'Purple Delight,' ×*Graptosedum* 'Vera Higgins,' and ×*Graptoveria* 'Opalina.' As you search your local garden centers, see if any of these variations on color, size, and shape appeal to you!

×*Graptoveria* 'Fantome'

Common names: Rock Rose, Mexican Snowball, Desert Rose

Rosette size: 3" (8cm) diameter

Stem size: 20" (50cm) long

Plants form distinct stems that are unable to retain the rosettes in an upright position and become creeping when grown on flat ground. The egg- to spatula-shaped succulent leaves of this ×*Graptoveria* are borne in dense, apical rosettes, and sometimes obscurely keeled below. They are light glaucous-gray and pink-infused in full sun. The leaf margins are a lighter, whitish blue color. The flowers, carried in diffuse inflorescences, are light yellow with the central section of the petals longitudinally light greenish infused.

As indicated by the multiplication sign that precedes the name ×*Graptoveria*, this is a hybrid between a species of *Echeveria* and a species of *Graptopetalum*. The parentage of the hybrid has been postulated as *Echeveria elegans* and *Graptopetalum paraguayense*.

CARE INSTRUCTIONS

Plants can be grown indoors in pots but really thrive outdoors.

Indoor care: Place plants kept in pots in a very well-lit area to best show off the blue-gray leaf color. Plants will also grow in low light, but then plants can become etiolated.

Outdoor care: Plants grow best where they are exposed to full sun. However, plants will also grow well in dappled shade.

Temperature: Plants are cold hardy to 20°F (-7°C).

Lighting: Strong light is preferable, but plants will also grow in dappled shade. In deep shade, they lose much of their charm.

Watering: Plants are very drought hardy and will grow perfectly well on irregular and very little irrigation.

Repotting: Potted plants can be kept in the same soil for many years. When repotting, cut off the stems and place a rosette on top of fresh soil. Roots will soon develop.

Propagating: Plants can be grown from stem cuttings and rosettes, as well as from leaves placed on top of the soil.

×*Graptoveria* 'Fred Ives'

Common name: Fred Ives Graptoveria, Giant Graptoveria

Stem size: 24" (60cm) long

Plants form clumps consisting of several stems that will creep along flat ground, dangle over the edge of a container, or spread across rocks in a rock garden. The stems are leafless, except toward the tips where the leaves are clustered into tight rosettes. Leaves are boat-shaped and slightly longitudinally keeled along the lower surface. Leaf color is blue green, but usually with a distinct pink, orange, yellow, or purple infusion. Flowers are pale yellow, and the upper parts of the carpels are red, giving the flowers a bicolored appearance.

Plants are known to form cristates, as shown here, with numerous rosettes developing along a flattened growing tip. As in the case ×*Graptoveria* 'Fantome,' ×*Graptoveria* 'Fred Ives' is also an intergeneric hybrid, with the parents having been given as *Graptopetalum paraguayense* and *Echeveria gibbiflora*.

🌱 CARE INSTRUCTIONS

Plants can be kept indoors in pots, but look their best when grown outdoors.

Indoor care: Keep plants in a brightly lit position.
Outdoor care: Plants are very easy in cultivation and one of the few succulents where the statement "flourish on neglect" is very accurate. Virtually the only maintenance required is, if long-stemmed plants are not desired, to refresh plants by cutting the rosettes off with a sharp knife or pair of pruning shears and placing them on the soil where plants are intended to grow.

Temperature: Plants are cold hardy to 20°F (-7°C).
Lighting: Exposure to several hours of direct sunlight per day is desirable to ensure that the plants look their best.
Watering: Plants need very little irrigation and take on an even more intense leaf color when under some stress. However, do not allow leaves to become dehydrated and shriveled.
Repotting: Plants can be kept in the same soil for many years. However, if short-stemmed rosettes are required, simply place a severed rosette on top of fresh soil in a pot.
Propagating: Plants can be easily grown from stems, rosettes, or individual leaves.

Hylotelephium cauticola

Common names: Stonecrop, Purple Stonecrop

Stem size: 10"–12" (15–30cm) long

Plants grow as small, upright to sprawling shrublets that consist of numerous, thin, purple-infused stems. The thin-succulent, egg-shaped to round leaves vary from bluish gray to strongly infused with purplish pink. Flowers, which vary in color from bright pink to deep purple, are usually carried in dense clusters.

Plants are perennial but deciduous. Numerous cultivars have been derived from *Hylotelephium cauticola* and from hybrids of which it is one parent.

CARE INSTRUCTIONS

Plants perform best when grown outdoors, but can also be kept indoors in pots.

Indoor care: Plants grow well in pots, but might lose some of the purple infusion if kept in low light conditions.

Outdoor care: Plants will do well if established in positions where they will receive several hours of sun per day, for example on a rockery.

Temperature: Plants are cold hardy and can be kept in temperatures as low as 25°F (-4°C), or even lower if the soil in which the plants are established remains dry.

Lighting: Plants prefer several hours of bright light per day.

Watering: Plants are very drought tolerant, but respond well to irrigation. Let the soil dry out before watering again.

Repotting: Plants benefit from being annually repotted. Remove a plant from its pot, divide it, and plant in fresh soil.

Propagating: Plants produce (underground) rhizomes and can be multiplied by dividing the shrublets.

Hylotelephium 'Herbstfreude'

Common names: Herbstfreude, Autumn Joy

Size: 24" (60cm) tall and wide

Plants grow as upright, deciduous, clumping shrubs that consist of grayish green, branched, leafy stems. Leaves are also grayish green, and round to oval in outline, and quite large. Leaf margins are softly scalloped into tooth-like crenations. The small, star-shaped flowers are borne tightly congested in flat-topped to slightly rounded inflorescences. During a flowering season, flower color changes from pink to deep red.

This is one of the largest-growing cultivars of *Hylotelephium*, and plants are very conspicuous when planted in large drifts, or even singly, in a garden bed. It is also popular in industrial-sized landscaping projects because of its ease of cultivation and low-maintenance requirements. Plants are deciduous in winter, leaving only the upright, brownish, dehydrated inflorescences. Many gardeners leave these in place as they add a further level of interest to a winter garden. Although it is often regarded as having been derived from *Hylotelephium telephium* only, it is of hybrid origin, with the latter species and *Hylotelephium spectabile* as parents.

CARE INSTRUCTIONS

Plants can be kept indoors in pots, but grow best outdoors in open beds or in pots.

Indoor care: Keep pots in bright light.

Outdoor care: Plants require little care once established.

Temperature: Plants are cold hardy and can tolerate temperatures as low as 25°F (-4°C)

Lighting: Full sun or dappled shade.

Watering: Plants are drought tolerant, but will also respond well to drenching the soil regularly.

Repotting: Repot after plants are spent. Plants do well in poor soil.

Propagating: Plants can be divided in spring or stem cuttings can be taken in summer.

Hylotelephium spectabile

Common name: Showy Stonecrop, Iceplant

Size: 24" (60cm) tall and wide

Plants have succulent stems along which the generally light green leaves are arranged alternately or in whorled clusters. The thin-succulent leaves are spoon-shaped and quite large. Leaf margins are usually shallowly scalloped, especially toward the tip, but can also be smooth. The star-shaped flowers are densely arranged in flat-topped to slightly rounded clusters. Flower color varies from white to pink to purple, depending on the origin of the material, or which cultivar is grown. The stamens overtop the flowers and at a distance give the inflorescences a furry appearance.

This species is exceptionally useful for planting in borders. Plants, also when in flower, remain more or less the same height, producing broad swathes of color in a garden. An extensive range of cultivars have been selected from *Hylotelephium spectabile* as well as from hybrids of which it is one parent. The flower color of these ranges from snow white to various shades of pink and purple. In very warm climates, plants have been noticed to suffer from heat damage to the leaves.

CARE INSTRUCTIONS

Plants grow very well outside in open beds in a garden, for example in a large meadow, but can also be kept indoors or outdoors in pots.
Indoor care: Keep the pots in bright light. However, plants really come into their own when grown outdoors.

Outdoor care: This is a hardy species that presents very little trouble when grown outdoors in open beds.
Temperature: Plants are cold hardy to 25°F (-4°C).
Lighting: Full sun or dappled shade.
Watering: Plants respond well to regular irrigation. Make sure the soil is well drained.
Repotting: Plants can be lifted annually or biennially and planted in fresh soil.
Propagating: Propagate by dividing clumps.

Hylotelephium telephium subsp. *telephium*

Common name: Orpine, Live-Forever

Size: 18" (45cm) tall

Plants are haphazard, mound-shaped succulents that can be densely or sparsely branched. Leaves are succulent, purplish-infused, oval to egg-shaped in outline, and the margins are adorned with blunt-tipped crenations. Ball-shaped clusters of reddish, pinkish, or yellowish-white flowers are produced in late-summer and early-autumn.

A multitude of selections and hybrids of *Hylotelephium telephium* subsp. *telephium* are available in the horticultural trade. Plants are deciduous; once dry, they can be trimmed or the dehydrated inflorescences can be left on the plants for extra interest in the garden.

CARE INSTRUCTIONS

Plants grow well outdoors in open beds and in pots, and pots also can be kept indoors.

Indoor care: Keep plants in brightly lit positions.

Outdoor care: Despite its ability to grow in moist positions, plants should not be planted where the soil remains waterlogged.

Temperature: Plants are cold hardy to 25°F (-4°C).

Lighting: Plants grow well in full sun and in dappled shade.

Watering: If plants are kept in pots, the soil should be allowed to dry out before follow-up watering is applied. In well-drained open beds, plants can take quite high rainfall without the risk of root rot setting in.

Repotting: Plants can be repotted at the beginning of the growing season.

Propagating: Plants can be propagated by dividing a clump or by stem cuttings.

Hylotelephium 'Vera Jameson'

Common names: Vera Jameson, Purple Stonecrop

Size: 12" (30cm) tall and wide

Plants grow as small, variously rounded shrublets, with the thin stems often arching and drooping. Leaves are round to oval-shaped and cover most of the length of a stem. The stems and leaves rapidly take on an opulent purple color, for which this cultivar is famous. Flowers are star-shaped, dusty to dark pink, and carried in short, often diffuse clusters at the tips of the branches. Plants of *Hylotelephium* 'Vera Jameson' are deciduous in winter. Stems can be trimmed back in early spring.

CARE INSTRUCTIONS

Plants can be kept indoors in pots but look their best when exposed to bright sunlight.

Indoor care: Keep the pots in bright light.

Outdoor care: Plants grow well outdoors and are well suited for use as edging in a border or on a rockery. Plants do well in dry positions and even in poor soil. They will also respond well to being grown in a trough or window box.

Temperature: Plants are hardy to 20°F (-7°C).

Lighting: Plants do best in bright light.

Watering: Plants are drought hardy and need only be watered once the soil has dried out.

Repotting: Plants benefit from being replanted into fresh soil on an annual basis.

Propagating: Propagation is through dividing a clump or by taking softwood cuttings.

Orostachys boehmeri

Common names: Dunce Cap, White Spikes

Size: 1"–3" (2.5–7.5cm)

These are small plants that have their leaves clustered into tidy rosettes. The leaves are bluish green and round tipped. Numerous thin stolons arise from between the leaves; these carry small plantlets at the tip. White flowers are densely arranged in uprightly held flower spikes. Given the rapid formation of plantlets through stolon development, plants will rapidly fill up a pot. Eventually the stolon-borne plantlets will cascade over the rim of a pot.

CARE INSTRUCTIONS

Plants will grow well in pots kept indoors or outdoors.

Indoor care: Keep plants in a brightly lit position and do not overwater the plants.

Outdoor care: Given the small stature of the rosettes, they do very well in pots kept in full sun or in dappled shade.

Temperature: Plants are cold tolerant to 20°F (-7°C).

Lighting: Plants can grow in full sun and in dappled shade. In deep shade, the tidy, compact rosettes lose some of their charm.

Watering: Water once a week, but ensure that the soil is well drained.

Repotting: Plants can be profitably repotted once a year. The species seems to relish being regularly provided with fresh soil.

Propagating: The plantlets borne at the tips of the stolons can be removed with a pair of scissors and planted on.

Petrosedum sediforme

**Common names: Pale Stonecrop,
Bushy Petrosedum**

Stem size: 10"–12" (25–30cm) long

Plants grow as small, dense, multistemmed shrublets. Stems remain upright, become leaning with age, or sometimes even drooping under the weight of the leaves that are often restricted to the upper half to third of the stems. Leaves are succulent and shaped like short, thick pine needles. Leaf color varies, from the most common bluish green to strongly pink- or yellow-infused. Light yellow flowers are carried in densely-flowered, upright inflorescences.

The branch tips sometimes become crested— horizontally flattened—with numerous small rosettes developing on the edge of the flattened growing point, which will add interest to any succulent collection. Because the stems resemble miniature pine trees, they can be profitably established in bonsai pots to create miniature landscapes.

CARE INSTRUCTIONS

Plants will grow outdoors in open beds or in pots, or indoors in pots.

Indoor care: Place the pots in which the plants are kept in a sunny position. Make sure the potting soil is well draining.

Outdoor care: Plants do well outdoors in a sunny spot in, for example, a rockery. Plants established in pots should be placed in a sunny position.

Temperature: Plants are cold hardy to 28°F (-2°C).

Lighting: Strong sunlight brings out the best leaf colors.

Watering: *Petrosedum sediforme* originates from the Mediterranean basin of Europe. When cultivated, it responds well to wet winters and hot, dry summers.

Repotting: Plants can be repotted into fresh soil every two years. However, plants have also been known to grow happily in the same soil for many years.

Propagating: Stem cuttings of 1"–2" (2.5–5cm) long will easily strike root.

ECHEVERIA

If you want classic rosette-shaped plants to keep in pots or fill out your display, look no further than the genus *Echeveria*. The variety in this group is as dramatic as could be wished for, and you'll fall in love with these fat-leaved, ornamental beauties. With a few exceptions, all echeverias are easy in cultivation.

Echeveria affinis

Common name: Black Knight, Black Echeveria

Size: 6" (15cm) diameter

Plants develop low-growing rosettes that are borne atop short, stout stems. Once old leaves have withered, they are shed, yielding a clean stem with conspicuous leaf scars. The sharp-tipped, boat-shaped leaves that taper to both ends are light to mid-green but most often have a nearly uniform black infusion. Flowers are carried on rather short, branched, robust inflorescence stalks and are bright red. The often nearly black rosettes and bright red flowers are the main attractions of this species.

CARE INSTRUCTIONS
Plants do well outdoors in full sun as well as indoors in pots in bright positions.

Indoor care: Place plants in a brightly lit spot and do not overwater them.

Outdoor care: Plants do very well if grown in a pot placed in bright sunlight. Rosettes can also be planted in a rockery.

Temperature: Plants can tolerate temperatures of as low as 20°F (-7°C).

Lighting: Plants do best in bright light, and if grown outdoors will benefit from as many hours as possible of direct sunlight.

Watering: Plants are drought tolerant and only need to be irrigated once the soil in which they are cultivated has dried out.

Repotting: Plants benefit from being repotted into fresh soil every two years. If low-growing rosettes are desired, simply cut the rosette off the stem, allow the wound to dry, and place it on top of the fresh soil.

Propagating: Plants usually remain solitary for many years before starting to form clumps. These lateral sprouts can be removed and grown on.

Echeveria agavoides

Common names: Lipstick Echeveria, Agave Echeveria, Century Plant Echeveria, Waxy Echeveria

Size: 6" (15cm) diameter

Plants develop into low-growing rosettes that remain stemless for a long time, especially in cultivation, before developing a short trunk clothed in old, dry leaves. Leaves are light to mid-green, and the leaf margins of the horticulturally most desirable variants are often red infused. The leaves are short triangles to elongated boat shaped. Red flowers with yellow mouths are carried sparsely in inflorescences of which the upper part droop gracefully.

Plants take on the shape of miniature century plants—representatives of the genus *Agave*—hence some of the common names that reference those spiky plants. However, unlike most agaves, the leaf tips of *Echeveria agavoides* are not pungent.

🌱 CARE INSTRUCTIONS

Plants do exceptionally well outdoors, but can also be grown indoors in harsh climates.
Indoor care: Keep plants in bright light conditions and do not overwater them.
Outdoor care: When grown outdoors, plants do slightly better in Mediterranean-type climates where the winters are cool and wet and the summers are hot and dry. However, most variants of the species will also grow happily in summer- or all-year-rainfall regions if the soil is well drained.
Temperature: Plants can tolerate 20°F (-7°C).

Lighting: Plants thrive in brightly lit positions.
Watering: Plants are very drought tolerant and should only be watered once the soil in which they are grown has dried out.
Repotting: Plants do not mind becoming pot bound for a few years, but will benefit from being repotted every two years.
Propagating: Once a rosette has started to form a clump, remove the side shoots, and grow them on.

> *Echeveria* has spawned countless cultivars, hybrids, and selections that vary wildly in color, size, and shape. *Echeveria agavoides* alone has numerous names applied to a range of selections, such as 'Lipstick' and 'Ebony.' Most require similar care, but always double check gardening experts (in centers and online) for each new selection to ensure it lives a long time.

Echeveria 'Big Red'

Common names: Big Red, Red Echeveria

Size: 10"–12" (15–30cm) diameter

Plants grow as large rosettes that will nicely fill a pot with a diameter of 12" (30cm). Plants do not develop a stem as rapidly as some other echeveria hybrids and cultivars. The leaves are large spatulate and a light green color with a reddish margin. However, in bright light the leaves turn a vivid, luminescent red. Large, pinkish to bright red flowers are borne on

arched inflorescences. As with similar species, such as *Kalanchoe sexangularis*, the attraction of *Echeveria* 'Big Red' is the intense red color of the leaves.

CARE INSTRUCTIONS

Plants do very well if grown outdoors, but can also be cultivated in pots kept indoors.

Indoor care: Place plants in brightly lit positions.

Outdoor care: Plants do well in pots kept outdoors, or as filler in a rockery.

Temperature: Plants ideally should be kept above 41°F (5°C).

Lighting: Bright light is preferable.

Watering: Plants do best if watered regularly once the soil in which they are grown has dried out. If the soil in which plants are grown is well drained, they will tolerate very high levels of rainfall.

Repotting: Plants can be repotted every two years, but like many succulents, remain looking very good if slightly pot bound.

Propagating: If the growing tip is removed, the remaining stem will develop side shoots that can be cut off with a pair of pruning shears or sharp knife and planted on, after allowing the cut ends to dry in the shade for a few days.

Echeveria 'Doris Taylor'

Common name: Doris Taylor, Hairy Echeveria, Wool Rose

Stem size: 6"–7" (15–18cm) tall

Plants grow as small rosettes that are carried at the top of upright stems. The light to mid-green, spatula-shaped leaves are densely covered in short, white hairs. The hairy leaves are very attractive and the main reason why this cultivar is popular in cultivation. The rather large flowers are predominantly yellow, but with distinct orange or red infusion, and clustered in upright to slightly leaning inflorescences.

CARE INSTRUCTIONS

Plants do very well when grown outdoors in bright sun, but will also grow indoors in pots.

Indoor care: Plants look their best when exposed to good light.

Outdoor care: Plants do exceptionally well in pots and will in time develop short stems.

Temperature: Plants should be kept at a temperature above 40°F (5°C).

Lighting: Keep plants in well-lit places.

Watering: Plants are drought hardy and only need to be watered once the soil in which they are grown has dried out.

Repotting: Plants can be repotted into fresh soil every two years. However, plants will grow well in the same soil and container for many years.

Propagating: Remove branch cuttings and basal sprouts with a sharp knife and root them in fresh soil. The same can be done with the terminal rosette.

Echeveria elegans

Common name: Snowball Plant, Mexican Gem

Size: 4" (10cm) tall

Plants grow as small rosettes that are stemless or short-stemmed, and multiply freely. The egg- to spatula-shaped leaves vary somewhat in color but are generally pale blue-green to almost white—hence the common name Snowball Plant. Flowers are dusky pinkish red lower down and yellow or greenish yellow toward the mouth. The flowers are borne on arched stalks. With its tight rosettes this is one of the ideal echeverias to grow in a pot.

CARE INSTRUCTIONS

Plants grow well outside in bright light, either in full sun or in dappled shade.

Indoor care: Plants can be kept indoors, but make sure that they receive bright light.

Outdoor care: Plants do very well if grown in pots kept outside. The dappled shade on a patio is also perfect for growing the plants.

Temperature: Below 32°F (0°C), plants generally show frost damage.

Lighting: Full sun or dappled shade.

Watering: Plants must not remain in waterlogged soil. Rather, let the soil dry out between watering events.

Repotting: Plants can be repotted once they have filled up a pot.

Propagating: Propagate plants by dividing a clump. Plant each rosette in fresh soil in a small pot.

Echeveria gibbiflora

Common name: Giant Echeveria, Roof Shingles

Size: 12"–18" (30–45cm) tall

Plants produce open rosettes at the tips of generally sturdy stems that can become leaning with age. The large spatulate leaves vary from light green to more bluish gray, often with pinkish hues, and tend to be longitudinally folded upward. Flowers are pink on the inside to bright red externally. The flowers are carried on tall, upright inflorescences that can reach a length of 36" (1m).

Echeveria gibbiflora has been used as one of the parents of a multitude of hybrids from which what must be hundreds of cultivars have been selected. Variegated-leaved variants are known as well as plants that develop unnatural-looking outgrowths or blisters on, especially, the upper leaf surface. This feature, however, is not to everybody's liking.

CARE INSTRUCTIONS

Plants do best outdoors in strong sunlight, but can also be grown indoors.

Indoor care: Keep plants in a place that receives bright light.

Outdoor care: Plants should be grown in bright sunlight but will also perform well in dappled shade.

Temperature: Plants are hardy to around 32°F (0°C).

Lighting: Plants do best in bright sun.

Watering: Allow the soil to dry out between watering events.

Repotting: Plants will grow happily in the same soil for many years. Repotting can be done after three to four years.

Propagating: Plants can resprout from leaves, but this is not always a failsafe method for *Echeveria gibbiflora*. Stem cuttings work best.

Echeveria lilacina

Common name: Ghost Echeveria, Spooky Echeveria

Size: 5"–6" (13–15cm) tall

Rosette size: 10" (25cm) diameter

Plants produce low-growing, symmetrical rosettes that will in time develop short stems that become leaning, given the size of the large rosettes. The ball-shaped to flattened rosettes consist of numerous spoon-shaped to almost square or rectangular leaves that end in a pointed tip. Leaves are thick, succulent, a very pleasant nearly white to light blue color, and have a distinctly waxy appearance. Inflorescences are downcurved to rolled upward toward the tips. Flowers are urn-shaped, quite large, and pale pink to coral red.

This is a strikingly beautiful echeveria. Although slow growing, it has visually very pleasing, compact rosettes.

CARE INSTRUCTIONS

Plants grow very well outdoors in bright, sunny positions. Plants can also be kept indoors but need bright light to look their best.

Indoor care: Keep plants in bright light.

Outdoor care: Plants grow well in full sun. Under such conditions, the leaves take on a light lilac coloration.

Temperature: Plants are hardy to around 40°F (5°C).

Lighting: Full sun or dappled shade.

Watering: Let the soil dry out before rewatering.

Repotting: Plants can remain in the same pot for several years before repotting.

Propagating: Plants can be propagated by dividing plants that have developed multiple rosettes. Leaves can also be rooted.

Echeveria 'Moondust'

Common name: Moondust Echeveria

Size: 9" (23cm) tall and wide

Plants will remain as large, single rosettes for a long time, but with age, might develop some offsets from the base to form a closely packed group of one large and a few smaller rosettes. The thick, fleshy leaves are pale bluish—from a distance they appear almost white—and covered in a waxy bloom that easily rubs off. Single or double, downcurved to almost coiled inflorescences are produced prolifically at any time of the year. The flowers are dusky pink to orange infused.

This is a hybrid between *Echeveria laui* and *E. lilacina*, and one of the most prolific flowerers of all echeverias. Plants can produce up to seven inflorescences simultaneously or in quick succession and always seem to be in bloom. The soup plate–sized rosettes of *Echeveria* 'Moondust' consist of numerous fat, curved-in leaves—a very attractive plant to grow.

CARE INSTRUCTIONS

Plants thrive outdoors, but can also be kept indoors in pots.

Indoor care: Keep plants in pots in brightly lit positions.

Outdoor care: This is one of the easiest echeverias to grow. Simply plant them in well-drained soil, place the pots in full sun, water occasionally, and they will grow very well.

Temperature: Plants do not show frost damage to 22°F (-5°C).

Lighting: Plants must be given bright light—ideally several hours of full sun per day.

Watering: Plants are very drought tolerant. Allow the soil in which plants are grown to dry out completely before rewatering.

Repotting: Plants have been known to happily grow in the same pot and soil for more than 10 years.

Propagating: Plants that have formed clumps can be divided. However, plants are best grown from the bract leaves that develop on an inflorescence.

Echeveria purpusorum

Size: 2"–3" (5–7cm) tall

Plants resemble small aloes or agaves in that their sharp-tipped leaves are borne in tight, usually solitary, rosettes. The thick, triangular leaves appear brownish because of numerous small flecks on a light to khaki green background and terminate in harmless tips. Flowers are borne sparsely on an elongated, arching inflorescence. The urn-shaped flowers are red with yellow apices. With its thick, succulent, rosulately arranged leaves tightly packed in small clusters, *Echeveria purpusorum* is a very desirable species to grow.

🖐 CARE INSTRUCTIONS

Plants look their best when grown outdoors in bright sunlight.

Indoor care: Place plants in brightly lit positions.

Outdoor care: Plants thrive if given several hours of full sun per day. The soil in which they are grown must be well drained.

Temperature: Plants can tolerate temperatures of just below 32°F (0°C).

Lighting: Plants need to be exposed to bright light to look their best.

Watering: Plants are very drought tolerant, and the soil in which they are grown should be allowed to dry out before watering.

Repotting: Plants can remain in the same pot for several years. However, plants respond well to biennial repotting into fresh soil.

Propagating: Old, well-established plants will produce side shoots from the main rosette; these can be removed and planted on. Somewhat surprisingly, many clones of *Echeveria purpusorum* do not grow easily from severed leaves, no matter how carefully they are removed from a rosette. Rather, seed-sowing is a useful way of producing more plants.

The bright flowers of *Echeveria purpusorum* contrast beautifully against the dark leaves.

KALANCHOE

Known for both their flowers and their spectacular leaves, kalanchoes, which belong in the family Crassulaceae, will add color and texture to your home, garden, or succulent craft.

Kalanchoe beharensis

Common names: Donkey's Ears, Aureo-aeneus, Baby's Bottom, Brown Dwarf, Feltbush, Minima, Napoleon's Hat, Pixel, Subnuda

Size: Up to 9' (3m) tall

Plants grow as large shrubs or small trees, but remain much smaller when kept in a small pot. They have twisted stems and branches that prominently display the pointed scars where leaves were shed. Leaves are furry—rarely smooth, as in Baby's Bottom and Subnuda—with the color of the fur being grayish green, yellowish, or brown. The leaves are scalloped along their margins and shaped like small or large arrowheads, hence the common name Napoleon's Hat. Inflorescences are carried on side branches (not at the tips of the stems and branches as is the case in most kalanchoes). Flowers are dull yellowish green with prominent, longitudinal purplish stripes on the corollas. The corollas can be tightly twisted downward.

A large range of variants of *K. beharensis* have been selected for the horticultural trade. Some of these are hybrids; for example, *K. ×edwardii* 'Fang,' which has *K. beharensis* and *K. tomentosa* as parents.

Almost all the selections have furry leaves, but a few, such as *K. beharensis* 'Baby's Bottom,' are completely smooth at maturity.

CARE INSTRUCTIONS

Best grown outdoors, but can be kept indoors for many years if grown in a container.

Indoor care: Place in a pot in a well-lit area.

Outdoor care: Plants grow very easily in a range of soil types and require minimal care and irrigation.

Temperature: At 32°F (0°C) the leaves and growing tips are severely damaged.

Lighting: Plants need bright light.

Watering: Plants are very drought hardy and will grow well on minimal irrigation. They can also take a lot of rainfall with no ill effect when grown outdoors in open beds.

Repotting: Plants can be kept in a small container for many years. This will stunt their growth and turn them into interesting bonsai trees.

Propagating: Plants can be easily grown from stem and branch cuttings, as well as from leaves, or even pieces of leaves—just place the leaves on top of (not in) the soil; it will soon strike root and develop small plantlets, especially at the cut end. Stems and branches should be placed in the soil, directly where they are intended to grow.

Kalanchoe blossfeldiana and Selections

Common names: Flaming Katy, Florist's Kalanchoe, Widow's Thrill

Size: 5"–8" (12–20cm) tall

FEATURED SELECTIONS AND HYBIRDS:
- *Kalanchoe blossfeldiana* 'Calandiva'
- *Kalanchoe blossfeldiana* 'Else Flower'

Plants grow as small, generally mound-shaped, shrublets that carry oppositely arranged, large, dark green leaves along green—later grayish brown, somewhat corky—stems and branches. Inflorescences are usually densely packed with single or double flowers. Flowers can be virtually any color of the rainbow, except blue.

Globally, *Kalanchoe blossfeldiana* is the most important succulent in the horticultural trade for indoor plants. Store-bought plants will last for several weeks or even a few months, and flowers are similarly very long lasting.

CARE INSTRUCTIONS

This is an indoor succulent. Plants can be placed outside for brief spells—an hour or two per day—but do not grow well when left outside.

Indoor care: Keep plants away from places that receive too much sun, which will likely damage the leaves.

Temperature: Plants are not cold hardy and should be kept at temperatures higher than 41°F (5°C).

Lighting: Plants thrive in low to bright light conditions. In direct sunlight plants can easily become scorched.

Watering: Pots should be watered regularly, and the soil should not be allowed to dry out completely. Watering should be done by placing pots in a large saucer filled with water, rather than from the top, to prevent spoiling the flowers and water drying on the leaves, leaving unsightly marks.

Repotting: Once plants have flowered, this material is ready for the compost heap. This is not a repeat flowerer.

Propagating: Replace material with new plants purchased from a florist or nursery.

Kalanchoe blossfeldiana in pink and yellow

Kalanchoe blossfeldiana 'Calandiva'

Kalanchoe blossfeldiana 'Else Flower'

Kalanchoe bracteata

Common names: Silver Spoons, Ghost Kalanchoe

Size: 48" (1.2m) tall and wide

Plants grow into haphazardly rounded shrubs with numerous, horizontally flexed branches. The leaves are round to oval in outline and a ghostly white to silvery color—hence the common names. The leaves have a felty texture. On older leaves, the felty layer will in time rub off, exposing a light green surface. Flowers are bright red to dusty pink in color. With its ghostly white leaves and contrasting red flowers, this is a very desirable species to grow.

CARE INSTRUCTIONS

Plants do best outdoors but small cuttings can be planted in small containers and kept indoors for several years.

Indoor care: Keep plants in bright light.

Outdoor care: If grown outdoors, plants perform best when given bright, sunny positions, but will also grow well in dappled shade. In deep shade, plants will become etiolated.

Temperature: Plants can tolerate temperatures of around 32°F (0°C) for short spells.

Lighting: Plants need exposure to bright light to look their best.

Watering: Allow the soils in which plants are grown to dry out between watering.

Repotting: To obtain a large, shrubby specimen, repot into a pot one size larger than the one it is in on an annual or biennial basis.

Propagating: Plants grow easily from stem and branch cuttings, and leaves placed on top of the soil will easily strike root and develop new plantlets from the base.

Kalanchoe ×estrelae

Common names: Estrela's Kalanchoe, Fire Engine, Vivien

Size: 36" (1m) tall

Plants grow as robust specimens that have their opposite leaves arranged into what appears to be rosettes. The large, smooth-margined or very shallowly indented, paddle-shaped leaves are light green but usually heavily red or purple-red infused, especially in full sun. The pseudo-rosettes remain low growing to medium sized, but when flowering sets in, the plants elongate significantly. The small, cigar-shaped flowers are borne in dense clusters and have yellowish green tubes and white corolla lobes.

Kalanchoe ×estrelae is a hybrid between K. luciae and K. sexangularis. It shows considerable hybrid vigor, and in horticulture, easily competes with both parents in terms of attraction. The intense red color of the leaves is also enhanced when temperatures drop (but not to freezing) in winter.

⬡ CARE INSTRUCTIONS

Plants thrive outdoors, but can also be kept in a greenhouse.

Indoor care: Keep in bright light.

Outdoor care: Plant in a position that receives maximum sun for several hours per day.

Temperature: Plants can survive short spells of 32°F, but heavy frosts will kill them.

Lighting: Bright light.

Watering: Plants should be kept dry, but not completely dehydrated. The drier they are kept, the more intense the red coloration of the leaves.

Repotting: Plants that are kept in pots with a diameter of about 12" (30cm) will easily reach flowering maturity within two to three years.

Propagating: A plant that has flowered will die, but sprouts are produced from the base. These can be removed with a pair of pruning shears, left in the shade for a few days, and then planted directly in the soil where they are intended to grow.

Kalanchoe fedtschenkoi

Common names: Lavender Scallops, Shrub Kalanchoe

Size: 10"–12" (25–30cm) tall

Pictured is *Kalanchoe fedtschenkoi* 'Variegata,' which includes creamy to whitish-yellow around the margins. It is planted among some *Curio crassulifolius*.

Plants are low-growing shrubs that produce multiple stems that lean sideways under the weight of the upper, leafy stem and branch segments. This gives rise to large, irregularly mound-shaped specimens. Especially the stems that lean sideways produce stilt roots and, often, new plants on the stem at that point, and elsewhere along the stem. The flat, succulent leaves are oval to egg shaped in outline and a blue-green, orange, lavender, and even purplish color, hence the common name. The flowers, which are pendent, are borne in head-shaped clusters. Flower color varies from pink to orangey.

Nectar-sipping birds are attracted to the copiously nectariferous flowers. In mild climates, surplus material must not be discarded irresponsibly because they will easily become established and even somewhat weedy, especially in mild-climate places well away from the native geographical distribution range of the species in Madagascar.

⬡ CARE INSTRUCTIONS

Best grown outdoors, but plants can also be grown indoors in a brightly lit spot.

Indoor care: Keep plants in a place that receive bright light.

Outdoor care: Plants will easily grow in any soil type. A sunny position is preferable.

Temperature: Plants do not survive subzero temperatures.

Lighting: Well-lit areas.

Watering: Plants are very drought hardy, and will also easily survive if the soil in which they are grown is kept dry for long periods.

Repotting: Plants will happily grow in the same soil for many years. When repotted, use one pot size larger than the one in which the plants are grown.

Propagating: Propagation is from stem cuttings of any length that will root easily. Leaves, especially when severed from the stems and branches or are under other stress, will develop small plantlets in the notches on the scalloped leaves. These will root where they fall.

Kalanchoe sexangularis

Common names: Red Kalanchoe, Scarlet Scallops

Size: 12"–18" (30–40cm); when flowering, up to 40" (100cm)

Plants are medium-sized shrubs that will develop multiple, angled stems from ground level. The stems generally remain upright, but the tallest ones can become leaning. When the flowering event approaches in winter, the stems elongate to easily twice the height of nonflowering specimens, and multibranched inflorescences are carried at the branch extremities. The strongly red-infused to scarlet red leaves curve gracefully downward and are scalloped into blunt-tipped teeth. The inflorescences carry many small, yellow, tubular flowers.

This is one of the ultimate red plants. Except for the yellow flowers, all plant parts can be strongly bright red infused, or even uniformly scarlet. This species makes a striking, robust groundcover when established densely in a sunny place. Plants will also grow in shade, but then the red is diluted.

CARE INSTRUCTIONS

Plants grow best outside in open beds, but short stem cuttings can be easily grown indoors.
Indoor care: Keep plants in a very brightly lit spot to enhance the red leaf color.
Outdoor care: Plants should be established in a sunny place. Keeping irrigation to a minimum will further intensify the red color of the stems, leaves, and inflorescence branches.

Temperature: Plants are not cold hardy and must be protected when temperatures approach 32°F.
Lighting: Bright light.
Watering: Plants are very drought tolerant but will benefit from occasional irrigation.
Repotting: Plants can be kept in the same container for many years. Repot into fresh soil in the same-sized container, or one size larger.
Propagating: Plants are easy from seed and from stem cuttings.

Kalanchoe tomentosa

Common names: Bunny Ears, Chocolate Soldier, European Clone, Hairy Harry, Super Fuzzy

Size: 24"–30" (60–75cm) tall

Plants are small to medium and will ultimately develop into multibranched shrubs or shrublets, but will remain only a few inches tall for a long time if root growth is limited in a small container. All the plant parts are covered in a dense layer of short or long hairs that range in color from white to brown. The silvery white to dark brown leaves are generally sword-shaped and rather elongated, but a few selections have short, stubby leaves. Most variants of the species have brown spots, which could be confluent to make a continuous brown edge along the upper parts of the leaf margins. Flowers are greenish with a weak or strong purple infusion.

This is a very variable species, and a whole collection can be built up of the various leaf-color forms available.

CARE INSTRUCTIONS

Plants grow very well outdoors in mild climates and will also thrive indoors in a sunny spot.

Indoor care: Keep plants in a sunny spot.

Outdoor care: *Kalanchoe tomentosa* is very undemanding in cultivation and requires very little care. Plants look their best when grown in full sun.

Temperature: Plants can tolerate temperatures of around 32°F (0°C) for a short time, but prolonged exposure to such conditions will kill them.

Lighting: Bright light.

Watering: Allow the soil in which the plants are grown to dry out between watering. However, plants do not mind soil regularly being drenched as long as the growing medium is well drained.

Repotting: Plants can be grown in small containers for many years with no need for repotting. This will ensure that specimens remain small.

Propagating: Propagation is easy from stem cuttings of virtually any length, and leaves placed on top of the soil will sprout roots and plantlets from the base.

Kalanchoe tubiflora

Common names: Chandelier Plant, Mother-of-Millions

Size: 12"–24" (30–60cm)

Plants remain single-stemmed throughout their two- to three-year lifespans, and will only branch if the growing tip is damaged. The grayish green leaves are borne in whorls of three—which is uncommon in kalanchoe—around the stems. Leaves are cylindrical and about 1" (2.5cm) long. The stems elongate somewhat when flowering is initiated. Flowers are borne pendent and are carried in dense clusters. Flower color varies from bright orange to red.

Plants are not perennial and die after having flowered. However, *K. tubiflora* can easily become weedy when grown outdoors in mild climates and surplus material should not be discarded irresponsibly.

CARE INSTRUCTIONS

Plants grow will indoors and outdoors, but look their best outdoors.

Indoor care: Keep plants in bright light conditions.

Outdoor care: Plants grow with great ease in any situation and on almost any surface on which the roots can get a foothold. Plantlets that abscise from the leaf tips will root in very thin layers of soil, even in gutters, on roofs, and in joints between paving bricks.

Temperature: Plants prefer mild climates, but short cold spells with temperatures hovering around 32°F (0°C) can be tolerated.

Lighting: Strong light conditions are required to prevent plants from becoming etiolated and toppling over.

Watering: Very little irrigation is required.

Repotting: None required because plants are short lived.

Propagating: Propagation is from the multitude of plantlets that form at the tips of the leaves. These will strike root and grow where they fall.

SEDUM

While not every succulent in the genus *Sedum*, which belongs in the family Crassulaceae, bears leaves with a bean- to boat-like shape, most of the ones featured here have those types of leaves. That's because this unique shape makes for such a fun and unique addition to a group. You'll love these plants in a hanging pot or mixed in with a group. Some of these sedums are now included in segregate genera.

Phedimus spurius

Common names: Creeping Stonecrop, Red Carpet, Red Curtain, Caucasian Stonecrop

Size: 12" (30cm) tall

Plants grow as small, sprawling shrublets. Stems are rather weak and lean outward, creating a rounded, mound-shaped plant. The round, thin-succulent leaves are light green with the scalloped margins, often becoming red infused in good light conditions. Several variants with reddish purple or variously variegated leaves have been recorded and some of these are available in the horticultural trade under a range of monikers.

In very hot climates, *Phedimus spurius* should be protected against the heat. *Phedimus spurius* is sometimes still known under the name *Sedum spurium*.

🌱 CARE INSTRUCTIONS

Plants do very well outdoors if planted in dappled shade. Plants will grow well indoors.

Indoor care: Keep plants in bright, but filtered, light.

Outdoor care: Plants grow very well in pots filled with well-draining soil, if watered regularly. Plants can show some heat damage in very high temperatures. Plants do well when grown in window boxes or plant troughs where their stems will dangle over the edge of the containers.

Temperature: Plants are very cold hardy, tolerating temperatures easily to -4°F (-20°C).

Lighting: Plants do well in bright, filtered light. Especially if high solar irradiation leads to very hot conditions, plants will wither, and the leaves can become scorched.

Watering: Plants benefit from regular irrigation.

Repotting: Repot plants into fresh soil every two years.

Propagating: Plants can be grown from stem cuttings that root easily.

Sedum adolphi

Common names: Coppertone Sedum, Golden Glow

Stem size: 12" (30cm) long

Plants are many-branched shrubs, with sturdy stems and branches remaining uprightly disposed, leaning, or sprawling sideways. The boat-shaped leaves are about 1" (2.5cm) long and vary from light yellowish green to uniformly golden yellow, especially when plants are stressed. Leaves are closely packed toward the growing tip but more widely spaced lower down on a stem. The whitish flowers are tightly clustered in the ball-shaped inflorescences.

This is one of the easiest sedums to grow. It will ultimately develop into medium-sized shrubs, but if smaller plants are desired, regularly plant newly taken cuttings. *Sedum adolphi* is sometimes still known under the name *Sedum nussbaumerianum*.

CARE INSTRUCTIONS

Plants are ideally suited to outdoor cultivation, but can also be grown indoors.
Indoor care: Place pots in a brightly lit position or else the golden yellow leaves will lose much of their charm.
Outdoor care: For the leaves to take on the desirable golden yellow color for which the species is famous, full sun is required.
Temperature: Plants can grow outdoors in open beds in temperatures of slightly below 32°F (0°C).
Lighting: Bright light.

Watering: Plants are very drought tolerant and can survive on very little water. However, regular irrigation does them no harm and they also happily grow in soil kept moist, or even drenched for short spells.
Repotting: Plants can be repotted annually, but the easiest is to simply take cuttings and plant them in fresh soil.
Propagating: Place stem cuttings directly in the soil, in a pot, or an open bed where they are intended to grow. Roots will soon develop.

Sedum burrito

Common names: Donkey's Tail, Blunt-Tipped Donkey's Tail

Stem size: 36" (1m) long

This is one of the best succulents to grow in a hanging basket. Plants develop long, dangling stems tightly packed with succulent leaves. The stems will quickly cascade over the edge of a container. Leaves are short and stubby and terminate in a blunt tip. The leaves are bluish green and will take on a slight, yellow-infused color when grown in full sun. Leaf orientation is sideways rather than downward, as in *Sedum morganianum*. Deep pink flowers are borne in small inflorescences at the tips of the stems.

CARE INSTRUCTIONS

Plants grow well both indoors and outdoors.
Indoor care: Grow plants in a hanging basket in a sunny position.

Outdoor care: Plants are easy in outdoor cultivation and will rapidly produce a multitude of stems that should be allowed to cascade over the edge of a hanging basket.

Temperature: Plants can survive temperatures of around 32°F (0°C) for short spells. However, prolonged exposure to this temperature will cause frost damage, including excessive leaf drop.

Lighting: Plants look their best in strong light but will also grow well in dappled and even in deep shade. However, in shaded positions, the leaves become more widely spaced along the stems.

Watering: Plants are very drought hardy and only need to be watered once the soil in which they are grown has dried out.

Repotting: Plants can be repotted every two to three years, but this should be done with great care to prevent the leaves from becoming detached from the stems.

Propagating: Plants are propagated by stem cuttings of about 2" (5cm) long. Leaves placed on the soil will also sprout roots and plantlets.

Sedum clavatum

Common names: Aurora Blue, Blue Sedum

Size: 5" (12cm) tall, 8" (20cm) wide

Plants grow as small, branched shrublets. Branches initially remain upright, but will eventually sprawl sideways to form haphazardly rounded canopies. Stems are leafless lower down, with dense clusters of round to egg-shaped leaves tightly clustered

toward the stem tips. Flowers are bright white and borne in dense, rounded inflorescences. Given how the stems will eventually sprawl sideways, plants are well suited to being grown in hanging baskets.

CARE INSTRUCTIONS
Plants do well both indoors and outdoors.

Indoor care: Place plants in brightly lit positions.

Outdoor care: Plants grow well outdoors in full sun or in semi-shade.

Temperature: Plants are hardy to 32°F (0°C).

Lighting: Bright light.

Watering: Plants are drought tolerant, and soil should be allowed to dry out between irrigations.

Repotting: Repot plants biennially into fresh soil.

Propagating: Plants will easily grow from stem cuttings.

Sedum makinoi

Common names: Penny Plant, Tickey Sedum

Size: 2"–3" (5–8cm) tall

Plants develop into low mounds; when grown in a pot, the outermost stems become trailing. The stems are thin, generally weak, and do not remain upright once they elongate. Leaves are small, round, and flat, or very slightly folded downward along the margin—the common names are derived from the round, coin-shaped leaves. However, over the course of a year, leaves will vary from round to slightly more elongated and spatula-shaped, depending on the season. The leaves are shiny light green. Inflorescences are small and few-flowered while the flowers are very large for such small plants. Flower color is a diluted greenish yellow.

Plants available in the trade as *Sedum* 'Tundra Tornado' appear to be derived from *S. makinoi*; it could be a selection of the species or a hybrid of which *S. makinoi* is one parent. Selections of the species with a bronze color are the most popular in cultivation.

CARE INSTRUCTIONS

Plants can be grown indoors or outdoors.
Indoor care: When grown indoors, plants grow well in small to medium pots—a small specimen can even be planted in a 1" (2.5cm) pot where it will happily grow.
Outdoor care: Plants can be established as a groundcover in exposed positions.
Temperature: Plants do not show frost damage slightly below 32°F (0°C).
Lighting: Plants do best in bright light, which will enhance the shiny green color of the leaves. In some variants, the leaves will take on a bronzed color under such conditions.
Watering: Plants thrive on regular watering.
Repotting: Plants respond well to regular repotting into soil with a high organic content.
Propagating: Propagation is from stem cuttings that will root with ease.

Sedum morganianum

Common names: Burro's Tail, Sharp-Tipped Donkey's Tail

Stem size: 36" (1m) long

Plants develop long dangling stems. The stems are covered in short, cylindrical, blue-green leaves that are sharp-tipped, unlike the blunt-tipped leaves of *Sedum burrito*. The leaves point downward and not sideways. Flowers are burgundy red and carried in small clusters at the tips of the stems. Like *Sedum*

burrito, *Sedum morganianum* has the ideal growth form to serve as a hanging basket subject.

⬡ CARE INSTRUCTIONS

Plants thrive outdoors but can also be grown indoors.

Indoor care: Place plants in brightly lit positions and where there is space for the stems to dangle over the edge of a pot or hanging basket.

Outdoor care: Plants grow very well in full sun or in semi-shade.

Temperature: Plants will grow at temperatures as low as 32°F (0°C) without showing signs of frost damage.

Lighting: Plants perform at their best in bright light.

Watering: Only water plants once the soil in which they grow has dried out.

Repotting: Even when handled with extreme care, leaves very easily become dislodged from the stems. Rather than attempting to repot them, which will almost invariably leave parts of the stems exposed and devoid of leaves, take stem cuttings that can be established in fresh soil in a new hanging basket.

Propagating: Plants grow easily from stem cuttings of virtually any length. Leaves placed on top of the soil will root and develop new plantlets.

Sedum pachyphyllum

Common names: Jelly Bean Plant, Jelly Baby, Finger Sedum

Stem size: 12" (30cm) long

Plants grow as small to medium shrubs that develop numerous stems that variously remain upright, lean sideways, or become sprawling. Jellybean- to small-club-shaped leaves are carried along the upper parts of the branches. Leaf color varies from light green to bluish green and the upper parts of the leaves are often intensely red. Small, yellow, star-shaped flowers are produced in small, dense clusters. Plants need very little care once they are established in open beds or in pots.

CARE INSTRUCTIONS

Plants will grow indoors and outdoors, but look their best when grown outside in full sun.

Indoor care: Place plants in very well-lit positions.

Outdoor care: Plants thrive in bright sunlight, either in pots or in open beds.

Temperature: Plants show no frost damage at just below 32°F (0°C).

Lighting: The leaves become more widely spaced along the branches if plants are not kept in a bright, sunny position.

Watering: Plants are very drought tolerant, and soil should be left to dry completely between irrigations.

Repotting: Plants can be left in the same soil for several years. Rather than repotting, consider taking stem cuttings that can be planted into fresh soil, in open beds or in pots.

Propagating: Plants are easy to progagate from stem cuttings.

Sedum praealtum

Common names: Shrubby Sedum, Jade Sedum

Size: 36" (1m) tall

Plants grow into densely branched shrubs that take on a small, tree-like shape, but in cultivation are usually kept smaller. Numerous branches that spread sideways are produced, giving the plants somewhat rounded canopies. Leaves are spatula-shaped and a uniformly light green color. Small, yellow, star-shaped flowers are borne densely in cone-shaped inflorescences.

Plants can be readily trained into beautiful, medium-sized bonsai trees. The growth form and, to some extent, leaf shape of *Sedum praealtum* are similar to those of *Crassula ovata*, the jade plant, hence the common name jade sedum.

CARE INSTRUCTIONS

Plants can be grown indoors or outdoors.

Indoor care: Plants will grow well indoors if given bright light.

Outdoor care: Plants look their best when grown in the open in sunny positions. It will also grow in dappled shade.

Temperature: Plants should ideally be kept at temperatures above 32°F (0°C), but if damaged by frost, will usually resprout.

Lighting: Plants prefer bright light.

Watering: Plants are drought tolerant, but will also grow in heavy soils that retain moisture for a long time.

Repotting: Repot plants every two years.

Propagating: Plants are easily propagated from stem and branch cuttings that root with ease in virtually any soil type.

Sedum ×rubrotinctum

Common names: Jelly Bean Plant, Jelly Beans, Pork and Beans

Size: 2"–3" (5–8cm) tall

Plants grow as small shrublets that only reach a height of a few inches. However, given that the stems are quite weak, plants topple over and spread in width. The leaves are short-cylindrical and shaped like jellybeans, from which the common names are derived. Bright yellow flowers are produced in small clusters.

A variant of the red-leaved *Sedum ×rubrotinctum*, known as *Sedum ×rubrotinctum* 'Aurora' has pinkish to bluish leaves. It has been proposed that *S. ×rubrotinctum* resulted from a hybrid between *S. pachyphyllum* and *S. stahlii*.

Sedum xrubrotinctum

Sedum xrubrotinctum 'Aurora'

CARE INSTRUCTIONS

Plants can be grown indoors in small pots, or ideally, outdoors in full sun in open beds or in pots.

Indoor care: Keep plants in very brightly lit positions.

Outdoor care: Grow in full sun to ensure that the leaves take on the fantastic bright red color.

Temperature: Plants are not cold hardy and exposure to temperatures below 32°F (0°C) will almost invariably lead to mild or even severe frost damage.

Lighting: The higher the light intensity, the more pronounced the red infusion in the leaves.

Watering: Plants are very drought tolerant and only need to be irrigated once the soil in which they are grown has dried out. Drought stress will enhance the red leaf color.

Repotting: Repot plants with extreme care because the leaves become detached from the stems with great ease.

Propagating: Plants grow very easily from stem cuttings. The bean-shaped leaves can be placed on top of the soil where they will root and sprout new plants from the base.

SEMPERVIVUM

This genus of succulents, which is also included in the family Crassulaceae, is small but mighty, and especially sought-after because of their general cold hardiness. The iconic, multileaved and tightly packed rosettes make it unique from other similar growth forms. Plus, some standouts, like *Sempervivum arachnoideum*, bear remarkable features—robust inflorescences and large flowers, for example—that you won't find anywhere else.

Sempervivum arachnoideum

Common names: Cobweb Hens and Chicks, Cobweb Sempervivum, Cobweb Houseleek, Spider Web

Size: 1"–2" (2.5–5cm) tall

Plants produce a multitude of small, tight rosettes that, under good growing conditions, will rapidly fill up a container in need of an interesting groundcover. Leaves are light green and connected at their tips with white threads that give the rosette a cobweb-like appearance. Inflorescences are short but quite robust and bear several large, pink flowers.

Rosettes of *Sempervivum arachnoideum*, perhaps more than in other species of *Sempervivum*, tend to become cristate. This is where the apical growth of a rosette multiplies abnormally, for example in a horizontal direction to yield a half-moon-shaped apex.

CARE INSTRUCTIONS

Plants grow well outdoors as well as indoors. In both instances, they do best when kept in pots.

Indoor care: Keep plants in a well-lit position.

Outdoor care: Plants will grow very well in the open if kept in pots that receive full sun or dappled shade. Rosettes will grow well if used in a rockery where they can be placed in soil pockets between rocks. This will also help to keep their roots cool and the soil in which they are grown moist. In very hot climates, plants can become scorched. In such conditions, keeping them in dappled shade is preferable.

Temperature: Plants are very cold hardy and will survive temperatures of below 32°F (0°C).

Lighting: Plants grow well in dappled shade and full sun. In shady positions, the rosettes lose their compact growth.

Watering: Weekly watering is advised. The soil in which the plants are grown should be free draining and not become waterlogged.

Repotting: Plants that have flowered, which will occur within a year or two—sometimes longer—of their establishment, will die. It is best to, from the start, plant the rosettes in a container where the plants will not need repotting.

Propagating: A rosette will produce numerous offsets to the sides and on short stalks. These can be removed and planted on.

In a clump of tightly packed rosettes of *Sempervivum arachnoideum*, some will occasionally become cristate. Despite this mutation, the leaf tips remain connected with cobweb-like threads.

Sempervivum 'Ohio Burgundy'

Common names: Ohio Burgundy, Purple Sempervivum

Size: 2"–3" (5–8cm) tall

Plants grow as small rosettes that remain low growing; they reach a height of only a few inches. The leaves are spatula-shaped and end in a pointed but harmless tip. Leaves are variously finely hairy—sometimes hardly so—and a reddish to purple color, which is the great attraction of the plants. Leaf color is enhanced in brightly lit positions and during cold spells. The large flowers are pink.

Plants can be planted densely and will quickly form a continuous purplish green to purple carpet. Make sure that the medium in which the plants are grown is well drained.

CARE INSTRUCTIONS

Plants grow very well outdoors in open beds or in pots, and can also be grown indoors in pots.
Indoor care: Keep plants in a place that receives a lot of sun.
Outdoor care: Plants will easily survive extremely low temperatures, for example when they are covered by snow. During the cold months the plants are dormant, with active growth resuming in spring and summer.
Temperature: Plants are very cold hardy and will easily survive freezing temperatures of -15°F (-26°C).

Lighting: If grown in full sun, the plants take on a beautiful purple color. Plants also grow well in dappled shade, but the leaf color will be diluted.
Watering: Water plants weekly, or more regularly in the heat of summer. However, ensure that the soil is which plants are grown is well drained.
Repotting: Plants can be kept in small pots for a long time. When repotting, use the same pot size, but replace the soil.
Propagating: Plants develop new, perfectly formed rosettes on stolons. These can be removed with a pair of pruning shears and planted on.

Sempervivum tectorum

Common names: Common Houseleek, Hens and Chicks, Roof Houseleek

Size: 6" (15cm) tall, 20" (50cm) wide

Plants are rosulate evergreens, with the leaves arranged in symmetrical clusters. In cultivation, plants usually remain small. The leaves spread outward during the seasons of active growth, and become curved in during the resting phase. Leaves are grayish green and often variously suffused with reddish purple, usually in the upper half and along the margins. The margins themselves carry very fine cilia. Flowers vary somewhat in color, from reddish purple to whitish pink, and are carried in small clusters on short but thick and robust inflorescence stalks.

The species is extremely variable, and literally hundreds of cultivars have been selected from it. These are often based on minute differences, for example in leaf color. Traditionally, *Sempervivum tectorum* are planted on house roofs to ward off evil.

CARE INSTRUCTIONS

Plants thrive outdoors in full sun, but can also be grown indoors in small pots.

Indoor care: Keep plants in a sunny position to encourage the purplish color of the leaves to intensify.

Outdoor care: Plants require very little care once established.

Temperature: Plants are extremely cold hardy and temperatures of well below 32°F (0°C) do them no harm. For this reason, this is likely the succulent most widely cultivated in Europe.

Lighting: Plants do well in direct sun and in dappled shade.

Watering: Plants benefit from regular irrigation, but are also very drought hardy. Their ability to grow in very thin soils means they are often found wedged between rocks or even placed on top of roof tiles.

Repotting: Individual rosettes that have flowered will die. It is therefore a good idea to establish them in pots that are large enough—about 5" (12cm) in diameter—for them to reach flowering maturity. Depending on the variant of the species being cultivated, plants will also flower if kept in smaller pots.

Propagating: Plants develop new, perfectly formed rosettes on stolons. These can be removed and planted on.

> *Sempervivum calcareum* is closely related to *Sempervivum tectorum*, meaning it is similar in appearance and care, and could easily be used as a replacement in succulent crafts.

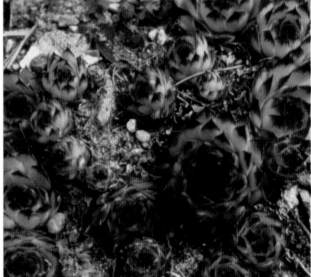

CARING FOR SUCCULENTS

A benefit to growing succulents is that they are very easy to establish and ultimately to keep in cultivation. Once well-rooted, they generally require almost no aftercare. For many species grown outdoors in suitable climates, little more is required than placing a cutting in the soil where it is intended to grow. Generally, almost no additional gardening attention is required other than to assure good soil drainage, good light, and some feeding; for example, occasionally add well-rotted compost to the soil.

Attention to a few basic horticultural rules will ensure that your succulents not only grow, but thrive.

KEEP THEIR FEET DRY

Although a few succulents prefer aquatic habitats, such as seasonal rock pools and marshy areas, the vast majority do not grow successfully in wet substrates.

Know when to water. Like most plants, succulents also have a resting phase during which they do not, or hardly, grow actively. During this time, they accumulate very little body mass. During this "dormant phase," care should be taken to not unnecessarily water succulents in containers or irrigate them in open beds. Plants that have their roots in waterlogged soil run the risk of losing their roots and succumbing to rot. The resting phase can be either winter or summer and, depending on from where the plants originate, watering should be kept to a minimum in either the warm or cold months. In other words, plants from summer-rainfall regions tend to not grow actively in the dry winter season. However, plants from winter-wet regions, such as Europe's Mediterranean regions, California's coast, and South Africa's Western Cape, tend to be dormant during the warm-to-hot summer months.

Kalanchoe thyrsiflora (center) cultivated in a concrete container in downtown Denver, Colorado, USA, in the Garden Block of the Denver Botanic Gardens. Note how the growing medium is friable and well-drained.

A seasonal succulent display wheel in the Missouri Botanical Garden, St. Louis, Missouri, USA. The plants here take on fantastic colors because of their exposure to direct sunlight in summer.

Maintain well-draining soil. In any collection of potted succulents, the easiest way to prevent plants from rotting is to ensure that the soil mixture is well-drained. Good drainage can be achieved in various ways, with the easiest being to add sufficient quantities of sharp, gritty sand to the mixture.

Avoid dehydration. Succulents do not necessarily thrive under conditions of extreme or even mild drought; they do need to be watered from time to time to look their best, especially when they are in an active growth cycle. Therefore, watering plants once the soil has become dehydrated is beneficial. Even a light watering during the dormant phase will not do succulents harm. Remember that growing plants in containers, and therefore restricting their root run, is an essentially artificial way of cultivating them.

ENSURE THEY RECEIVE SUFFICIENT LIGHT

Sufficient light does not equal exposing the plants to high loads of solar irradiation. In their natural habitats, succulents often start their lives as tiny plants in the shadows of non-succulent forbs, shrubs. When outdoors, succulents generally enjoy shade where sunlight is filtered through a sparse tree canopy. Because they don't receive as much sun during the day, most indoor succulents will be happy with bright light conditions, with slightly filtered light usually being sufficient.

SUCCULENTS BENEFIT FROM FEEDING

Especially when succulents are grown in containers, the soil will eventually be depleted of the nutrients required for normal growth. Providing plants with occasional feeding will substantially improve their growth. Unlike plants growing in their natural habitats, or even in open beds, pot-bound plants do not benefit from the influx of nutrients derived from decaying organic material. Healthy, well-grown and -fed plants have the further benefit that they tend to better cope with the few pests that attack succulents.

Propagation

Many succulents have evolved multiple mechanisms for reproduction. These various mechanisms can be broadly classified as either **sexual reproduction** or **vegetative reproduction**—the latter also being referred to as asexual reproduction. The benefit of vegetative reproduction is that the offspring is genetically identical to the mother plant from which the material was derived. Therefore, if you have a particularly striking plant that you would like to multiply, such as a variegated-leaved agave that sprouts from the base, removing these sprouts (also called "pups") from the mother plant and growing them on will generally assure you a batch of new plants that are similarly and attractively variegated.

The most common mechanisms through which succulents can be augmented are by sowing seed (sexual reproduction), or by taking cuttings of various organs (vegetative reproduction), such as stems, roots, or leaves.

PROPAGATING FROM STEM CUTTINGS

Rooting the cuttings from succulents is a very easy way to increase the number of plants in a collection and is likely the method beginners will be most comfortable with trying. Fortunately, most branching succulents are exceptionally suited to this means of propagation. Material severed from a mother plant can be virtually any shape or size, provided that the cutting has sufficient reserves to survive a short period without the rooted plant from which it was removed.

A distinct benefit of propagating plants from cuttings or even truncheons (large stems or branches) is that quite large plants can be rapidly obtained directly in the spot where they are intended to grow in a garden. There is no better way to obtain a mature-looking border of shrubby or tree aloes or columnar cacti, for example.

Here are some guidelines on taking and rooting stem cuttings:

- **Cut a branch or rosette as cleanly as possible** from as close as possible to the main stem or branches of the mother plant. Use a pair of pruning shears.
- If the stem of the cutting is too long or unwieldy, **cut it to the desired length**.

This potted specimen of *Agave lophantha* 'Quadricolor' has been root-bound in a small container. Each of the basal sprouts can be removed, trimmed of redundant growth, and planted.

- Dip the cut end of the stem to be rooted in commercially available **rooting hormone powder**. For most succulents this is not necessary, as most cuttings will soon put out roots with no particular stimulation required. However, the hormone powder prevents the cutting from rotting while it is not yet in the soil.
- **Let the wound dry** by leaving the cutting in the shade for a few days—not more than a week.
- Once the wound is dry, small cuttings can be placed in a **well-draining soil mixture**, such as sharp river sand supplemented with sifted compost.
- **Keep the growing medium moist** but not waterlogged.
- The cuttings will **soon develop roots**.
- Large cuttings can be **placed and staked in an upright position** directly in the spot where they are intended to grow.
- Established cuttings benefit from a well-draining medium being placed at the bottom of the planting hole to **prevent them from "standing" in waterlogged soil**.
- In beds in the open, newly planted cuttings should be **watered sparingly** until they show signs of growth.

PROPAGATING FROM ROOTS AND RHIZOMES

This is not a common method of propagating succulents. However, some species will indeed develop new plants if a root is removed and planted on. In some cases, a plant forms **rhizomes**, which are stems that resemble roots and grow horizontally often just below the soil surface or somewhat deeper in the soil.

Carefully remove the rhizome from the soil and plant it in the desired position. Place the portion that was underground below the soil surface again; keep the part from which a new plant will develop at or just above soil level.

PROPAGATING FROM LEAVES

Not all succulents will grow from severed leaves. The leaves of aloes, for example, will not root regardless of how much care is used to remove it from the mother plant. However, the closely related gasterias and many haworthias will easily grow from leaves.

Fortunately, many echeverias and sedums in the Crassulaceae, the stonecrop family, which are very adaptable and popular in succulent crafts, are also easy to propagate from leaves. Or in some cases, they are propagated from the bracts (small leaves) on the peduncle that carries the inflorescence.

Some guidelines:

- **Carefully remove a few leaves from the stem**. In many instances, it is ideally removed with some of the material that the leaf is attached to the stem with, remaining intact.
- This is achieved easiest by **removing the leaves by hand** rather than with a knife or pruning shears.
- **Place the leaves on top of the growing medium**, such as a well-draining soil mixture sifted into a seedling tray.
- **It is not necessary to insert the leaf into the soil**. In fact, doing so will likely lead to the leaf rotting within days.
- **Keep the tray away from direct sunlight** to prevent the leaves or bracts from becoming rapidly withered.
- The leaves will **soon develop roots** that will anchor the leaf or bract as well as the small rosette that will form opposite to the roots.

This rhizome developed from a plant of *Agave tequilana* that has finished flowering and died (agaves will flower once before dying). The green bud developed below soil level. The rhizome can be planted by covering it with a layer of soil, with the developing rosette exposed aboveground.

The spectacularly beautiful *Echeveria* 'Moondust,' a selection of a hybrid between *Echeveria laui* and *Echeveria lilacina*, can be easily propagated by placing bracts removed from the peduncle on top of—not in—a suitable soil mixture. The bracts will soon develop roots and small rosettes.

The plantlets forming on the margin of the *Kalanchoe serrata* leaves can be removed and placed on a suitable growing medium. Within a season or two, the plantlets will reach flowering maturity.

A tray of *Kalanchoe brachyloba* seedlings. Note that the seed germinated in two waves. Some seedlings are ready to be transplanted, while others have just emerged.

PROPAGATING FROM PLANTLETS DEVELOPING ON LEAVES

Some species form small but perfectly formed plantlets, also called bulbils or buds, on the margins of their leaves. The easiest way of propagating these succulents is by simply removing the plantlets and placing them on top of the soil in a seedling tray. These usually grow rapidly and could even flower within a growing season or two.

PROPAGATING FROM SEED

Most species require cross-pollination to produce viable seeds, which means at least two specimens should flower simultaneously, with viable pollen transferred from the anthers of one plant to the receptive stigmas of another. If pollination, followed by fertilization, was successful, fruit will be produced. Once ripe, a crop of seeds will become available. Some species are self-compatible and will produce seeds even in the absence of a second, or several, individuals of that species being in flower.

If multiple compatible species flower at the same time, for example in a greenhouse, it will be best to isolate the plants that you would like to cross-pollinate and from which a batch of seed is required. Many species are quite promiscuous, accepting pollen and producing viable seeds when crossed with other species or even with species from other genera.

As a rule of thumb for best germination results, seeds should be sown shortly after they were harvested. Fresh seeds generally germinate more readily and rapidly than seeds that have been stored for a period. However, in some cases, seeds several years old will also germinate.

Some guidelines:

- **Fill a seedling tray** to about ½" (1cm) from the top with a suitable soil mixture that has been sifted into the tray and lightly patted down.
- **Spread the seeds** as evenly as possible on the soil surface.
- **Cover large seeds** with a thin layer of sifted, sandy soil.
- **Very fine seeds do not need to be covered** as this may hamper or even prevent germination.
- **Place the tray on a large saucer filled with water** so it is watered from the bottom. This prevents the soil, seed, and topsoil from being washed away.
- Once germination has taken place, seedlings can succumb to damping off, which is a fungal attack. To prevent this, a **commercially available fungicide** can be added to the water.
- Seedlings derived from densely sowed seeds will soon fill the tray. When they have about four to eight leaves, depending on the species, the **seedlings can be planted** in the place they are intended to grow or into individual containers.

WHY CRAFT WITH SUCCULENTS?

One of the reasons succulents became so popular is that they are easy to maintain in a variety of displays. Terrariums are the most common and popular way of displaying succulents. But it just takes some experimenting to realize that these plants can thrive outside of the flowerpot. With the proper care, succulents can be incorporated into topiaries, wall hangings, and bouquets. The only thing better than a painting of nature is a painting made of living plants. There are so many possibilities with this medium that you can easily decorate your home, your garden, and even yourself with succulents!

It's important to remember that these pieces are not permanent. Succulents grow and will require repotting. However, if you create a proper base, then new plants can then be placed, and your crafts can live on.

THINGS TO KEEP IN MIND WHEN STARTING YOUR SUCCULENT CRAFTS:

- Each project will provide the succulent varieties used in the example craft. However, feel free to use this as a guidepost, and **utilize whatever succulents you have on hand** or in your local nursery. If succulents are not readily available in your location, do a quick online search to find almost any variety, shipped directly from nurseries to your front door!

- Most of the projects in this book use a combination of whole succulents and cuttings. You can use either or both. Keep in mind that **cuttings are sometimes easier** to work with when crafting living topiaries, succulent crowns, etc. Before you get started, prepare your cutting selections by trimming them to about a ½"–1" (1.3–2.5cm) stem and letting the cut callus (harden) for 1–2 days. This helps the cutting to not get root rot when it is placed in damp moss or soil.

- **Be creative with your color palette!** Crafting with succulents can be like choosing paint for an art piece or room. Compliment a turquoise room with purples, pinks, and greens; liven up a white or beige tabletop with bright splashes of color; or create a piece with complimentary colors or monochromatic pastels. The combinations are endless! Succulents truly come in all shapes, colors, textures, and sizes, so allow yourself to have fun with each project. No two creations are the same.

Having such a wide variety of succulents creates a lush and colorful craft.

GALLERY

In this book, you will find step-by-step instructions for creating truly unique, one-of-a-kind succulent projects and crafts. Before you begin crafting, get inspired by what other talented makers have created! This gallery showcases works from succulent enthusiasts, business owners, and DIYers that can give you ideas for designing and crafting your own original pieces using these hardy plants. From wedding accessories and Christmas decorations to charming accents for your home and garden, enjoy and be inspired!

Jessica Surface

AROSEZEN
Instagram, Facebook: Arosezen
Etsy: Arosezen
Malibu, CA

This birdhouse was crafted to create a mini paradise for our feathered friends in the garden. This project is a great place to use small baby succulents and off-shoots from your larger plants. Paint the birdhouse whatever color you prefer, then use hot glue to secure the moss and succulents to the roof. In addition to being visually pleasing, the moss and plants help to insulate the interior of the birdhouse, creating a cooler oasis in the summer and warmer climate in the winter.

This planter combines the raw beauty of an amethyst crystal with colorful live succulents. This planter, which was originally made to hold a tea light candle, is transformed into a gorgeous arrangement by adding a little soil and small succulent cuttings. Bright green moss is used to finish the display and create a stunning contrast to the natural deep purple of the crystal.

The naturally rugged beauty of driftwood makes the perfect planter for the wild yet structured look of succulents. This planter is made from driftwood collected from our local Malibu beach. After a thorough rinsing and drying out in the sun, the wood is hand carved out to create space to plant. Moss is secured around the larger edges of the opening using hot glue. This piece was designed as a Valentine's Day gift, so bright pinks and reds were used along with contrasting rich greens to create a romantic look. *Curio radicans* and *C. rowleyanus* spill out of the planter and cascade toward the edges of the wood for visual appeal.

Whimsical and fun, moss forms are one of my favorite ways to craft unique succulent artworks. This mini elephant was inspired by my trips to Thailand and their wonderful artistic depictions of elephants found in almost every street market stall. I planted a large pink Echeveria rosette at the center of the elephant's back to resemble a colorful saddle. Small succulents were used to create a face on the front of the elephant and accentuate the ears. *Curio crassulifolius* was used at the end of the trunk to give the appearance of the elephant spraying water, and a small cutting of *C. radicans* made for a cute little tail.

The perfect arrangement for the coffee or tea lover! This café-inspired piece is made by filling a wired metal teacup with sphagnum moss, a small amount of soil, and a variety of brightly colored succulents. The trailing plants are meant to be reminiscent of an overflowing cup. Create a similar look using an old tea pot with trailing plants coming out of the spout!

Caroline Sutton

Instagram: @LoveGrows.Plants
Southern California

I absolutely adore tiny things, especially tiny succulents. I was inspired to create my succulent Christmas tree because of a tiny terracotta pot. I used items from around my house, including sticks from my yard, floral foam, rocks, hot glue, and succulent clippings, to make a rustic and unique tree. As soon as I finished, I realized it was the perfect size to pair with another favorite of mine: my German incense smokers. The little Christmas gnome and my succulent tree decorated my entry way for months. When it was time to take it down, I removed the succulents easily and planted them in my yard. They grew roots right through the glue and continued to grow outside.

A good friend of mine (Lorin Paul, @something.gray) was making small, decorative Christmas trees out of concrete. Her use of concrete inspired me. As soon as I saw the silicone, gingerbread baking mold, I knew it would be the perfect size to make small concrete cottages. After the concrete dried, I white-washed them with watered down acrylic paint, glued a layer of moss to the top, and used craft glue to attach tiny succulent clippings. The succulents on these little houses can grow for months with proper lighting and water.

Diane Barnes

ARTFUL SUCCULENTS
www.ArtfulSucculents.com
Instagram: @ArtfulSucculentsLLC
Facebook: Artful Succulents
Etsy: ArtfulSucculents
Claremont, CA

These Christmas trees are made from driftwood from the shores of Lake Erie. I've added preserved mountain moss to the ends with a hi-temp glue gun. Then added are a collection of mini succulents, again using a high-temperature glue gun. The last piece of creating one of these is to pick the perfect succulent "star" for the top!

PHOTO BY ZACH TALIESIN (@ZACH_TALIESIN)

PHOTO BY ZACH TALIESIN (@ZACH_TALIESIN)

The succulents on this wreath are hand wrapped using 26-gauge wire attached to a 14" (36cm) metal frame. All the succulents are garden cuttings and the wreath after completion is approximately 18" (46cm). With minimal care, it can live up to a year!

This is one of my favorite projects to date! This resin gnome is a perfect palette for mini succulents! The "brim" of the hat and base are first sprayed with heavy-duty adhesive glue and then preserved mountain moss is attached. To help keep the hat portion secure, 26-gauge wire is tied around it. The mini succulents are then glued on using a high-temperature glue gun. A spritz of water every couple of weeks is enough to maintain this adorable gnome for months!

Flea market find! This vintage colander is first lined with sphagnum moss to cover the small existing holes, then succulent-mix soil and rooted succulents are added. Preserved mountain moss is added at the end to "tuck in" the plants and cover the soil!

This is another great flea market find! It's a vintage copper tea pot filled with succulent-mix soil then fully rooted succulents. I've added preserved mountain moss to tuck the plants in and keep them secure. The String of Bananas is used to mimic the liquid that this would have held when used for its original purpose!

James Mertke

THE SIMPLE SUCCULENT
Instagram: @The_Simple_Succulent
California

My arrangement creatively displays small succulents from an unusual perspective. It uses a half-submerged pot and decorative rocks to create the illusion of an upright planter.

Amanda Ryan

TERRACOTTA CORNER
www.TerracottaCorner.com
Instagram: @TerracottaCorner
Facebook: TerracottaCornerFL
Ocala, FL

Inspired by our favorite holiday trees, the Aurora and Alpine Succulent Trees can be enjoyed year-round and provide a whole succulent garden's worth of beautiful plants.

Jayme Waldt

STAYIN' ALIVE SUCCULENTS
www.StayinAliveSucculents.com
Instagram, Facebook, TikTok:
@StayinAliveSucculents
Fort Worth, TX

White fairytale pumpkin topped with colorful succulents. For this design we glue moss on top of the pumpkin (pumpkin is not carved into) and then attach a variety of succulents onto the moss with hot glue. All you have to do is spray the moss with water once a week to keep your succulents happy through the fall!

Mint fairytale pumpkin topped with colorful succulents. For this design, we glued moss on top of the pumpkin (pumpkin is not carved into) and then attached a variety of succulents onto the moss with hot glue. All you have to do is spray the moss with water once a week to keep your succulents happy through the fall!

Super fun black and gold miniature vintage sewing machine planter from Allen Designs filled with an assortment of colorful *Echeveria* and *Curio rowleyanus* .

PHOTO BY ALLEN DESIGNS STUDIO: WWW.ALLENDESIGNSSTUDIO.COM, @ALLENDESIGNSSTUDIO

Kileen Alvidrez

KILEEN'S GARDEN BOUTIQUE &
SUCCULENT NURSERY
www.SucculentVerticalGardens.com
Instagram: @KileensGardenBoutique
Clovis, CA

Experience the joy of vertical gardening! A great way to add a touch of greenery to outdoor fences, walls, entryways, or to an indoor sunny space, each frame is handmade, one at a time in our wood shop from reclaimed redwood and cedar. Every piece has its own unique characteristics and markings, with distinct knots and grooves, so no two frames are exactly the same! We artistically plant our vertical gardens with a variety of stunning succulents, such as sedums, so each arrangement is exclusively made. Succulent wall gardens require 4–6 hours of daily sunlight and water every 2–4 weeks.

We specialize in succulent vertical wall gardens in a variety of shapes and sizes. Urban redwood frames are handmade at our woodshop and planted with gorgeous succulents and *Sedums*, then shipped nationwide.

Mike Pyle

MIKE PYLE LANDSCAPE
DESIGN & CONSULTING
www.MikePyleDesign.com
Instagram: @MikePyleDesign
Orange County, CA

I designed this wall specifically for an "Eichler" home in Orange County using Ipe wood frames. I designed the pieces so that they would be away from the wall to add depth, as well as make room for backlighting.

The more the better! I always recommend planting succulent living walls as full as possible to get a dramatic outcome.

Mona Chin

THE SUCCULENT GARDENER
Instagram: @TheSucculentGardener and
@MonasSucculentsAndCrafts
California

This piece uses a Supermoss, 6" (15cm) Kokedama Planter, 32–38 of 2" (5cm) succulent echeveria heads, with or without roots, trailing succulents like *Othonna capensis* and *Curio rowleyanus*, potting soil, sheet moss, floral wire, and floral pins.

Made with a pinecone, succulent cuttings, and moss. Attach twine for hanging onto the pinecone before hot gluing moss onto the top of the pinecone. Select succulents that are proportional to the pinecone and hot glue the succulent cuttings onto the moss. Make sure the cuttings are held securely. It should be hung in a bright area, but away from direct hot sun. Spritz succulents every five days or so.

Using a birdcage of any size, sheet moss, potting soil, a selection of succulents. Shown in photo are propagated baby succulents. Poke holes into the sheet moss to plant succulents on the sides.

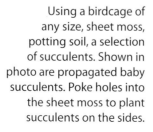

Using a wreath of any size or shape, Spanish Moss is attached onto the wreath with floral wire. Selected succulent cuttings are then attached onto the moss with either hot glue, floral pins, or floral wire, or a combination of the three to make sure the succulents stay onto the wreath. The wreath should be hung in a bright location, avoiding hot direct sun. Spritz the cuttings as needed till succulents start rooting, then wet the moss once it's rooted.

Choose a pumpkin of your choice, hot glue a circle of moss on top of the pumpkin. Make sure the moss is securely in place. Do not carve the pumpkin. Select succulents that are proportional to the pumpkin and hot glue them onto the moss. Use a variety of succulent of different texture, shapes, colors. Keep the height proportional and place succulents close and compact for a full look. Keep the pumpkin in a bright location but away from direct hot sun. Spritz the cuttings as needed till succulents start rooting, then wet the moss once it's rooted. Make sure to tip the pumpkin to remove excessive water and dry the bottom of the pumpkin to avoid rot. Succulents can be removed and replanted.

Toni Sicola

SUCCULENTS FOR HIRE
www.SucculentsForHire.com
Instagram, TikTok: @SucculentsForHire
Etsy: SucculentsForHire
Moab, Utah

The main thing I like to get across when I talk about my business is that succulents are a sustainable choice for wedding and event floral decor because they can be replanted after the party is over. All the succulents in my work are affixed or wrapped with care so that they can be replanted later. My clients receive care and replanting instructions so they can grow love gardens after they use their wearables at their events.

Nearly all the succulents in my combs and smaller pieces come from leaf propagation or small offsets off a mama plant. This one was for a bride who wanted to focus on greens and blues, so I mixed succulents with dried blue eryngium to complete the look.

This was the first comb I ever made, featuring tiny succulent rosettes from leaf propagation and fresh cut succulent flowers, which bloom in early summer where I live.

Using succulents and dried flowers can limit how big you go because of the weight (succulents) and brittleness (dried floral). But in this case, I was able to lengthen out the tiny dried white button flowers by placing them in afterward with hot glue and getting them to stick out and stand up just as I'd imagined.

These cuffs combined blues, pinks, greens, and whites to create a uniquely delicate style on thin silver cuffs. And the best part is that all the plants are affixed to felt that can be removed from the cuff, so the plants can be replanted and the cuff can still be worn later.

These copper cuffs were designed for guests of honor. Small pieces like this can make people feel included at your most special events. And the best part is that all the plants are affixed to felt that can be removed from the cuff, so the plants can be replanted and the cuff can still be worn later.

This is my take on wrist corsages in two different sizes. I combined pinks, greens, and dusty blues to achieve this look. And the best part is that all the plants are affixed to felt that can be removed from the cuff, so the plants can be replanted and the cuff can still be worn later.

To make these pieces, I first created a little felt disc that hooks over the leaves and hangs down so that I could avoid gluing directly to the leaves themselves. This way, when it's time to replant everything after a couple of months, the plants and felt can be removed and the leaf jewelry has a whole new life in your jewelry box.

This is one of the biggest statement rings I've ever made. It was for a special birthday gift and designed to look like it was growing up the wearer's hand. I used fresh sedum clavatum, other sedum, and crassula cuttings, along with succulent blooms from a giant echeveria hybrid.

Allison Reilly

DESIGNS BY ALLIE REILLY
www.designsbyalliereilly.com
Instagram: designsbyalliereilly
Lancaster, PA

Simple to make, this beautiful table centerpiece looks great all year round. By utilizing upcycled housewares, we are also able to limit our environmental impact. All you need is a banana hanger and a small pitcher!

This gorgeous take on a front door hanging sign combines the concepts of a wreath and a vertical garden! By adding a simple internal structure, this plant base is more secure. This can be personalized with a reversible family initial, or upcycle a fun baking tray to try different shapes.

This project combines upcycling, furniture design, and indoor gardening. This method is really easy but looks spectacular, and you'll want to upcycle all tables into living succulent gardens! Now all it needs is your favorite coffee table book.

WHAT YOU NEED TO GET STARTED

You may already have a lot of these supplies around your home! If not, all these basic supplies are easy to find at your local craft or hardware store and are budget friendly. In general, they're great to have on hand for other uses, too. It's also important to set up a proper workspace with a sturdy table, tablecloth if needed, and a roll of paper towels within reach. Succulent crafts can get quite messy!

WIRE CUTTERS

There are several kinds of wire cutters you can use, from floral wire cutters to a more heavy-duty pair of diagonal wire snips that have more cutting power. These might be your best bet so you can cut through any wire, no matter how thick it is. You can find them at any local hardware store.

WORK GLOVES

Some projects are simple and may not require gloves, but in other projects where you'll need to cut or shape wire, especially chicken wire, it's crucial to protect your hands so you avoid hurting yourself.

SCISSORS

A sturdy, high-quality pair of scissors is also a necessity for cutting tape, twine, ribbon, and other materials.

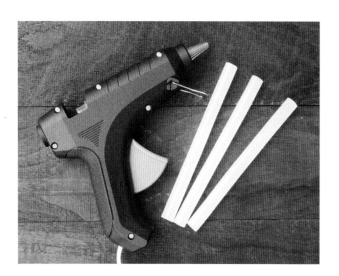

HOT GLUE GUN

A hot glue gun always comes in handy while crafting. It provides a hardworking glue that helps to secure elements, attach moss to disguise a greening pin, and more. Most importantly, it's perfect for attaching small succulents to your base. The glue won't hurt the plants, and their roots will easily grow around the spot of glue.

MEASURING TAPE

Because you'll be working with different kinds of wire that will range in size depending on the project, a measuring tape will work better than a standard ruler. It will also be useful when you install some of your finished pieces!

These small wire cutters are perfect for small arrangements. You'll need heavy-duty wire cutters for larger projects.

SCREWDRIVER

We'll be using a screwdriver for a few different purposes. In addition to fastening screws, it's also great for poking small holes into the moss when needed. Of course, you could always use a pencil or the tip of your finger, but a screwdriver is handy to have close by.

STAPLE GUN

A staple gun can be great for quickly and easily securing moss to certain projects. For this book, it will especially be helpful for the mirror project, vertical garden box planter, and more.

ELECTRIC DRILL

When combined with different bit sizes, a drill can easily create holes in a wood surface for attaching hooks, hangers, or screws. This is especially useful for when you want to attach your finished project to a wall or ceiling.

Craft Materials

These are materials that are geared for maintaining your succulents and making the crafts in this book. You can find these in your local garden center and hardware store. Make sure you follow any safety guidelines or instructions that come on the package to make the most of your materials.

MOSS

There are different kinds of moss, and I love using them all in my projects. I suggest keeping a little bit of everything on hand so you can see for yourself how they each add their own unique look and feel to your projects. And while there are many other types of moss easily available at craft stores and nurseries, these three are the main ones we'll be using and are a great place to start.

Sphagnum Moss

Great for retaining moisture and widely used for terrariums, sphagnum moss is a crafting favorite. It's great to work with, easy to find, and versatile. Because it doesn't get soggy, your succulents are less likely to have root rot issues, but with that in mind, waterings might need to be a bit more frequent than with soil. Its soft, light, and pliable form makes it easy to work with and pack into various shapes for display.

Forest Moss

Also called preserved moss, I love using forest moss to create a grassy look. It undergoes a very special process to retain its color, texture, and plush-like quality. Its durability makes it great for crafting, while also adding vibrant color and texture that's extremely low maintenance. Perfect for creating a finished look, it's a great choice to fill in empty spaces.

Reindeer Moss

Technically, reindeer moss isn't a moss but a lichen. Caribou, moose, and reindeer enjoy eating it, so that's how it got its name! It's bushy and has a sponge-like texture compared to other mosses you'll use, but because it grows in an off-white color, it makes it easy to dye and comes in a variety of different colors. Because such vibrant colors can be added to reindeer moss, it's perfect for adding eye-catching accents to your projects.

Sphagnum moss acts as a soil replacement.

Forest moss covers soil in a pleasing texture.

Reindeer moss adds colors and texture to any display.

WIRE

Depending on the project, different types of wire will be needed. We'll be using wire a lot to secure the plants together, especially when making topiaries, vertical gardens, bouquets, and other projects where succulents will need extra security to stay in place.

Chicken Wire

Durable and affordable, the possibilities are endless for using chicken wire in your crafts. It's a light wire netting that can be shaped, be easily molded, and will hold your moss and plants in place. Chicken wire is one of my go-to materials because of how versatile and sturdy it is. I recommend purchasing the 1" (2.5cm) hexagon wire because most succulent stems can easily fit in the spaces.

Floral Wire

Floral wire comes in several gauges, ranging from a thicker 16-gauge wire to a thinner 30-gauge wire. For the purposes of this book, we'll mostly be using 22-gauge floral wire.

Grapevine Wire

Grapevine covered wire is a great way to add a rustic aesthetic and texture to your projects. It's thicker and sturdier, but more decorative for projects where you won't need to hide it or cover it up completely.

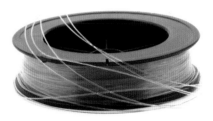

Fishing Line

Although it might not be what you think of when you hear the word "wire," this small but mighty material is perfect for securing succulents and other accents. Because it's clear, fishing line doesn't distract from the decorations you'll attach.

TWINE AND RIBBON

Whether it's adding a decorative bow for a flower crown or you're tying together a rustic-inspired bouquet, natural jute twine and colorful ribbon can finish off a piece and make it look amazing. While these can come in smaller rolls, I recommend buying a large skein if you want to do multiple projects.

PAINT

Acrylic Paint

Painting your projects with acrylic paint is a great way to add pops of color. Make sure to find nontoxic outdoor paint, since some of these crafts will be for your porch or garden and will need to withstand the elements.

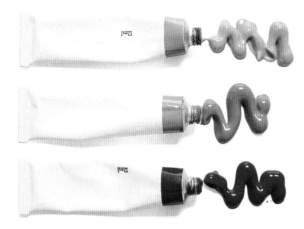

Wood Stain

Wood stains are perfect for finishing your planters and giving the wood a polished but natural look. Stains come in a range of colors, but whether you decide to stain or paint your project, make sure you give it plenty of time to properly dry before continuing on to the next steps.

Brushes & Water Cups

You can't use paints or wood stains without brushes. It also helps to have them in different sizes so you can add paints or stains on any surface, no matter how big or small. My tip is to have painting and staining brushes kept separate from each other for their specific use. Always keep a jar or cup of water nearby to easily clean off your brush, which will make it last for much longer.

FLORAL PINS

Also referred to as greening pins, mossing pins, or U-pins, these are simply used for attaching succulents, moss, and other materials to your base. They're made of wire that's similar to a paperclip, making them lightweight and easy to use.

When gathering your tools, it's handy to gather your succulents at the same time. That way, you can think through your arrangement and see what looks best together.

FLORAL PICKS

Floral picks are simply a thin wooden or metal dowel that acts as a flower stem. They're often used when crafting bouquets and are attached to the base of a succulent or faux flower with a dab of hot glue.

FLORAL TAPE

There are two main types of floral tape: clear floral tape and floral stem tape. In this book, we'll be using the floral stem tape (even though I'll be referring to it as "floral tape") and it usually comes in green, brown, black, and white at your local craft store. For the adhesive to activate, the tape needs to be stretched first. This is so the tape sticks to your project materials and not your fingers.

DIFFICULTY LEVELS

🌵	Beginner
🌵 🌵	Beginner-Intermediate
🌵 🌵 🌵	Intermediate
🌵 🌵 🌵 🌵	Intermediate–Advanced
🌵 🌵 🌵 🌵 🌵	Advanced

PROJECTS

Succulents are a perfect medium for a variety of crafts because they can grow in moss just as easily as dirt. Buying a premade moss ball or making a base yourself opens up a world of shapes, sizes, and orientations. These instructions will walk you through how to prepare your succulents, making the base for them to live in, and how to put it all together. Some projects can be made in a day, and will last for weeks or even months.

These projects are perfect for your home and garden, but there are some that work for special occasions, like a holiday or wedding. If you have the space for it, then these succulent projects can be enjoyed anywhere at any time.

LIVING SUCCULENT FAIRY GARDEN

 Beginner

This is a great project for children of all ages (and kids at heart)! At the end of crafting, each child can take home their very own magical fairy and succulent garden that will last for months to come. Our models and crafters for this project were Violet (age 12), Memi (age 10), Pearl (age 7), and Amelia (age 5). It's so much fun watching each child come up with their own unique creation.

MATERIALS NEEDED

- 6" (15cm) shallow terracotta pot
- Nontoxic outdoor acrylic paint
- Paint brushes
- Small palette
- Small containers or glasses of water
- Paper towels
- Well-draining succulent & cactus soil
- Fairy garden objects: mini animals, houses, fairies, unicorns
- Purple and green reindeer moss
- Decorations: rocks, crystals, pebbles, shells, etc.

SUCCULENTS USED

- Four 2" (5cm) succulent rosettes
- Variety of smaller clippings
- A few taller plants, such as *Crassula ovata* and *Kalanchoe ×edwardii* 'Rose Leaf'

For older kids or adults, you could also create a living Zen garden with mini figures, such as Buddha or angels, crystals, and colorful rocks or moss.

1. Place the pot upside down and paint the outside. Paint either one layer or let it dry in between coats if you want to create patterns. Dip your brush in water in between using different paint colors. You can also create your own colors by mixing them in the palette.

2. Let the outside of the pot dry. In the sunshine, it usually takes about 10–20 minutes. Flip the pot over and paint the top rim. You can also paint the entire inside of the pot. Let the inside dry.

3. Fill the pot with cactus & succulent soil.

4. Remove any dirt from the potted succulents. Gently massage the dirt away from the roots. You may need adult assistance for this part.

5. Start to create the mini fairy village.
Arrange the objects and crystals in the pot. After you figure out where you want things, then you can start to add in the succulents. It's also fine to plant the succulents first and add decorations after.

6. Arrange the succulents in the planter.
Make room for the new succulents by gently moving the soil out of the way with your finger or a pencil. Place the new succulent in the space you made and cover the roots with soil. Aesthetically, it can be nice to alternate colors and smaller varieties in between the larger rosettes. I like to plant the taller varieties in back of the planter, creating "trees" in a magical fairy scene.

7. Continue to arrange the garden by adding moss, rocks, shells, and whatever sparks your creativity. Once you are done, step back and enjoy your magical creation! Water the special arrangement and find a nice sunny spot for it in your home.

CARE
Water your plants once per week at nighttime or in the early morning. Water at the base of the succulents until soil is completely saturated and it runs out of the bottom drainage hole. Avoid getting water on top of the plants. Place the planter in a well-lit area with natural light for 4–6 hours a day (morning sunlight works best). If you see stretching, greening, or fading, the succulents need more light. When the plants eventually outgrow their fairy garden home, you can replant them into a larger pot.

LIVING SUCCULENT WREATH

 Beginner–Intermediate

Wreaths are the perfect statement piece for any season to decorate and liven up your front door or wall. Wreaths can also be used as a unique and interesting table decoration when laid flat and placed around candles or other centerpiece décor. Although wreaths can look complicated, they are actually quite simple to create. Making your own wreath gives you the flexibility to use the color palette you want and let your inner creativity shine through. These also make an excellent gift that will delight for months to come.

MATERIALS NEEDED

- 1 lb. (450g) bag sphagnum moss
- Large bowl or bucket of water
- 13" (33cm) wire wreath frame
- Scissors
- 120 ft. (36.5m) spool natural twine
- Floral pins
- Screwdriver or pencil
- Optional: Rooting powder
- Optional: Hot glue gun or tacky glue
- Optional: Wreath hanger

Note: To make this project easier, you can purchase a premade sphagnum wreath form instead of crafting your own. Soak the moss form in water for 10 minutes, then skip to step 6.

SUCCULENTS USED

- Ten 4" (10cm) succulents:
  - *Aeonium 'Kiwi'*
  - *Echeveria*
  - *Graptopetalum paraguayense*
- Eleven 2" (5cm) succulents:
  - *Sempervivum tectorum*
- Sixteen filler succulents with ½" (1cm) stems:
  - *Crassula ovata*
  - *Crassula rupestris*
  - *Sedum confusum*
  - *Sedum reflexum*

Wreaths can be customized for different holidays by choosing succulents and embellishments that complement the season. For example, decorate your wreath with a large gold or red ribbon for the holidays or with leaves and berries for the fall. Use red and pink varieties of plants or a heart-shaped wreath base for Valentine's Day and pastel colors for spring.

1. Gather the succulents and cuttings. Remove soil from rooted plants by gently massaging away the dirt. The larger plants will act as focal points. Let the cuttings harden for a day or so before using.

2. Fill a large bowl with water. Soak several handfuls of sphagnum moss for about 10 minutes. The moss will expand to five times its size when soaked in water. You can always add more moss to the water if needed.

3. Lay the wreath frame flat with the curved side facing up. Squeeze out excess water from the moss and place it around the wreath base. Use both of your hands to firmly squeeze the moss onto the wreath, molding around its shape.

4. Use twine to secure the moss. Cut about 10 ft. (3m) of twine. Wrap it around the entire wreath, leaving about two fingers' worth of space between each interval. Tie the twine firmly off on one end, then wrap it around the wreath base. Moss is messy and will fall off as you do this. If you lose too much moss while securing it, simply add more and keep going.

5. After wrapping twine around the entire wreath, tie it off. Repeat the process by cutting off more twine to wrap in the opposite direction. You want the twine to be wrapped tight enough to hold the moss in place but not so tight that you cannot fit the plants into the moss.

6. Arrange the succulents around the wreath. Let your creativity come out! Start with the statement succulents, such as the larger *Echeveria* rosettes. Fill in the rest of the wreath with the smaller varieties and fillers. When pleased with your design, either take a photo or carefully remove each succulent and place it to the side in the pattern you created.

7. Use a pencil or screwdriver to make a hole in the moss. Make it deep enough for the succulent stem or root to fit into. If you are using a cutting, you can dip the base in rooting powder before placing in the moss.

8. Place the stem or root into the hole. Secure the plant at its base with a floral pin. For larger succulents, you may need to use two floral pins. To use the pin, push it through the succulent root as close to the base as possible; secure it into the moss and under or around the twine. A hot glue gun can be helpful for securing smaller varieties that do not have a ½" (1cm) root base. Glue can also be used in place of the floral pins, but it is not as secure for holding the larger rosettes.

9. Continue arranging the succulents around the wreath until it is filled with plants and most of the moss is hidden. Take a step back and note any areas that could aesthetically use more filler succulents and add in as needed. Trim off any excess moss hanging off the bottom or sides of the wreath to give it a cleaner look.

10. Hang the wreath with more twine. Create a loop to tie around the metal base at the top. You can also use a metal wreath hanger by simply fastening it under the wire base at the back. If the wreath is to be placed on a door, lay it flat for a few weeks to allow the plants to root themselves and become more secure before hanging.

CARE

Place the wreath where it will get 4–6 hours of bright, indirect sunlight. You don't want to place it where it will get too much sun as this can burn the leaves of the plants. Bring the wreath inside if there is threat of frost. When the moss is dried out, usually every other week, water the wreath by submerging it. You may need to water it as much as once per week in a hot, dry climate. Once the succulents outgrow the wreath (usually about 6 months), they can be replanted in soil. Your wreath can then be refreshed by adding fresh cuttings!

PUMPKIN TOPIARY

 Beginner–Intermediate

These colorful pumpkins make the perfect decor for Halloween and the autumn season. They are fun yet simple to create. Your living pumpkin can be placed on your front stoop or displayed as a colorful centerpiece on your harvest table. The base of the living pumpkin is a moss ball, found readily online and at craft stores in all sizes.

MATERIALS NEEDED

- 6"–7" (15–18cm) premade moss ball
- 4" x ½" (10 x 1cm) stick for stem
- Large bowl of water
- Towel(s)
- Scissors
- Natural twine
- Floral pins
- Hot glue gun
- Screwdriver or pencil

SUCCULENTS USED

- 2" (5cm) succulents:
  - *Aeonium* 'Kiwi'
  - *Echeveria* 'Melaco'
  - *Echeveria* 'Blue Rose'
  - *Graptopetalum paraguayense*
  - ×*Graptoveria* 'Opalina'
  - *Sempervivum* 'Ohio Burgundy'
  - *Sedum clavatum*
- Small filler succulents:
  - *Sedum rubrotinctum* 'Aurora'
  - *Graptopetalum paraguayense*
  - *Sedum morganianum*
  - *Echeveria harmsii* 'Ruby Slippers'
  - *Crassula ovata*
  - *Crassula rupestris*
  - *Curio rowleyanus*

Use succulents with autumnal colors like reds, oranges, and yellows, to embrace the pumpkin look. By excluding the wooden "stem" element, this piece could easily be adapted into a centerpiece for any time of year.

1. **Prepare your succulents by removing all soil.** Succulent cuttings should sit for 1–2 days prior to placing in the wet moss. Your stems should be between ½"–1" (1–2.5cm) with leaves carefully removed. If your succulent does not have a stem, you can secure it with a floral pin. Soak your moss ball in a large bowl of water for about 30 minutes before beginning your project.

2. **Remove the ball from the water.** Create a pumpkin shape by flattening out your wet moss ball using your hand. This is going to release a lot of water, so place a towel or two underneath. Using the palms of your hands press down on the ball until it is about 2" (5cm) flatter.

3. **Create the lines of your pumpkin.** Cut 24" (61cm) of twine and wrap it around your pumpkin from the top to bottom. Cross underneath and bring it back to the top, like tying a ribbon on a present. Pull tightly and secure the twine by tying a double knot on top. Cut another length of twine and repeat to create the other sections of your pumpkin. When you are done, the pumpkin will have eight sections.

4. **Trim off any excess twine.** Leave two knots on top your pumpkin. Create a hole on top of the pumpkin. This is for the "pumpkin stem." Use your fingers or a screwdriver to make a space in between the twine.

5. Fill the hole you made with hot glue. Insert your stick for the pumpkin stem.

6. Arrange your succulents until you find a design you like. Start at the top of the pumpkin with your larger plants, then expand down with smaller and trailing succulents. I did not fill in the whole moss ball so the pumpkin shape can show at the bottom. When you are ready to begin planting, make your first hole in the moss. Use a pointy tool, such as a pencil or screwdriver.

7. Place hot glue in the hole that you made. Insert the stem of the succulent in the hole you made. You can also use floral pins instead of the hot glue to secure your succulents. Repeat this step for the rest of your succulents.

8. Plant trailing succulents. Hide the base underneath the leaves of a larger plant. Take a step back and fill in bare areas with smaller succulents.

CARE

Place in an area that receives bright, indirect sunlight. Water when moss is completely dried out. This should be about once per week depending on the humidity in your area. To water, simply submerge in water for about 5 minutes. When the fall season is over, you can remove your succulents from the pumpkin and plant them in a pot with well-draining soil. Your pumpkin can be saved and reused for next year.

CHRISTMAS TREE TOPIARY

 Beginner–Intermediate

Create a gorgeous topiary Christmas tree for the holiday season! This colorful succulent decoration can be used as a centerpiece or to bring some festive color to entryways, side tables, or an outdoor patio. Chicken wire is surprisingly easy to craft into a cone, making this a great project for beginners. This tree is 18" (46cm) tall and meant to impress with a colorful array of succulents in several varieties. Modify your measurements when cutting the chicken wire to make your tree smaller or larger, based on your needs. This tree looks great on its own, but you could place it on a base to give it some extra height.

MATERIALS NEEDED
- 20" x 24" (51 x 61cm) chicken wire
- Wire cutters
- Gloves
- Floral pins
- 1 lb. (450g) bale sphagnum moss
- Large bucket of water
- Hot glue gun
- Optional: LED fairy lights
- Optional: Needle-nose pliers

SUCCULENTS USED
- Two hundred 2" (5cm) succulents and cuttings:
  - *Sedum clavatum*
  - *Aeonium* 'Kiwi'
  - *Crassula perforata* subsp. *perforata*
  - *Echeveria* 'Blue Atoll'
  - *Echeveria* 'Hawaii'
  - *Graptopetalum paraguayense*
  - *Graptopetalum* 'Superbum'
  - *×Graptosedum* 'Vera Higgins'
  - *×Graptoveria* 'Opalina'
  - *Echeveria* 'Melaco'
  - *Sedum ×rubrotinctum*
- Star on top of tree:
  - *Sedum adolphi*
- Base of tree:
  - *Echeveria harmsii* 'Ruby Slippers'
  - *Crassula ovata* 'Dwarf Jade Plant'
  - *Crassula ovata* 'Curly Jade'

Using plenty of greens and reds makes this perfect for Christmas. To add even more cheer, you can wrap your tree in LED fairy lights to make it glow. Instead of the yellow succulents, add a star to the top.

1. Remove any soil or leaves from the base of succulents and cuttings. Let cuttings sit for 1–2 days prior to placing in the wet moss.

2. Cut chicken wire using the wire cutters. Use the border of the wire as the top and bottom of the Christmas tree. If you want a larger or smaller tree, adjust the size you cut accordingly. Chicken wire is very sharp, so always wear work gloves when handling.

3. Start to roll the chicken wire into a cone shape. The point end of the cone will overlap more than the bottom part.

4. Fold the wires together in the ends you cut. Use the fingers or needle-nose pliers to twist them together. Use wire cutters to trim any excess wire sticking out.

5. Continue shaping and trimming the wire until you have a symmetrical cone shape. Keep the bottom of the cone open so you can add in the moss. When you've finished the initial tree form, it will be about 27" (69cm) high. It will be shorter after filling the form with moss and folding in the bottom to create a base.

6. Soak the sphagnum moss. Place in a large bucket of water for about 10 minutes. It will expand to about 10 times its size.

7. Use your hands to squeeze out excess water from the sphagnum moss. Pack it into the tree tightly against the wire. When you place the first handful of moss on the top, pack it tightly to create a nice full shape. Fill up the form until there is about 9" (23cm) of wire left at the base.

8. Close the base of the topiary form. Fold in the bottom of the chicken wire like you are wrapping a present. Do about three folds to create a flat base. Trim excess wire as needed. Twist wires together to hold them in place.

9. Shape the cone. Use your hands to even out any unsymmetrical sides.

10. Start planting the tree. Use your finger or a pointy device to make a hole in the base of the moss form. Put a small amount of hot glue into the hole. This will secure the succulent stem to the base, and it will not hurt the plant.

11. Continue planting the tree. Alternate colors and varieties until you have the look you like. I start with larger rosettes, then fill in empty spots with smaller succulents. Attach the larger succulents to the base with floral pins. Make a hole in the form, pierce the base of the stem with a floral pin, and secure it to the moss form.

12. Place smaller cuttings in between bare spots to give the tree a fuller look. Occasionally take a step back to look at the tree and see what colors and plants it needs. For smaller plants with tiny stems, it is easier to use hot glue to hold them in place.

13. Create a succulent star for the top of the tree. Use three small cuttings from 4" (10cm) containers to create a star-like effect. To make it more durable, use a hot glue gun to hold it in place.

14. Create the base of the tree with larger green succulents. This gives the base of the tree a fuller look and adds some nice green color and body to the topiary.

CARE

Place in an area that receives bright, indirect sunlight. Water when moss is completely dried out. This should be about once every 10–14 days in the winter months. To water, simply submerge for 5 minutes or use a spray bottle with a directed spay throughout to drench the tree. After the holiday season or when the succulents begin to grow out of the arrangement, gently remove them from the base and plant them in soil. Your topiary form can be reused next holiday season.

GROOM & GROOMSMAN BOUTONNIERES

 Beginner–Intermediate

These are so simple to create and bring a distinctive touch to traditional wedding or prom attire. Succulents and flowers can be coordinated to match dress colors. For a wedding, the groom's boutonniere can be made to complement the bridal bouquet.

As a bonus, these instructions cover both a groom's boutonniere as well as some options for the groomsmen. Try these two different styles, one with a more rustic feel utilizing twine, and one with a more traditional look with a white ribbon.

MATERIALS NEEDED

- 22-gauge floral wire
- Floral tape
- Ribbon or twine
- Hot glue gun
- Boutonniere pin

SUCCULENTS AND PLANTS USED (FOR GROOM)

- 2" (5cm) *Echeveria* rosette
- *Echeveria harmsii* 'Ruby Slippers'
- *Crassula arborescens* subsp. *arborescens*
- Silver Dollar Eucalyptus

SUCCULENTS AND PLANTS USED (FOR GROOMSMAN)

- 2" (5cm) *Echeveria* rosette
- *Crassula rupestris*
- *Crassula perforata* subsp. *perforata*
- *Crassula rubricaulis*
- Silver Dollar Eucalyptus
- Ursula Purple Thistle
- Baby's Breath

Groomsman

Succulents add a structured and unique look to the traditional groom's boutonniere.

Groom

1. Prepare cut flowers and leaves. Cut stems to about 3" (7.5cm) long. Remove any soil from rooted plants by gently massaging away the dirt. Arrange the succulents and filler plants to your liking.

Groomsman | Groom

2. Create the succulent stems. Cut 6" (15cm) of floral wire using wire cutters. Pierce the stem or the stub at the base of the succulent plant and bring the wire through to the other side. Pull the wire until the ends are even and in a U shape, facing downward. Gently twist the wires together to form a stem. Repeat with any succulents that have a stem less than 1" (2.5cm) long.

Groomsman | Groom

3. Wrap each stem with floral tape. Gently pull the floral tape to activate its "stickiness." Start at the top of the stem by the base of the succulents. Wrap the floral tape in a spiral downward until you reach the base of the stem. Use your fingers to pinch the tape as you go to help it stick to itself.

Groomsman | Groom

4. Rearrange the filler plants around the succulents. Secure the filler plants to the rest of the arrangement with floral tape. If you like the look of the boutonniere with just the green floral tape, you can finish at this step!

Groomsman

Groom

5. Secure the ribbon or twine. Use hot glue at the top of the floral tape near the base of the plants. Spot on a small amount on the back of the boutonniere. Carefully place the cut end of the ribbon or twine on the glue. Be careful not to burn your fingers on the hot glue.

Groomsman

Groom

6. Tightly wrap to the bottom of the piece. If any of the stem is still showing or it looks uneven, you can do a second wrap from the bottom back up. Once you finish wrapping, use another spot of glue on the back of the stem to secure the ribbon or twine. Secure boutonniere with a pin.

CARE

Succulent boutonnieres can be made a few days before your event. If you are incorporating fresh flowers, make it the day before or day of to keep it looking fresh. Plant the succulents when you are finished with the boutonniere by carefully removing the plants from the floral tape and wire, then planting in well-draining soil.

BRIDE & BRIDESMAID BOUQUETS

 Intermediate

Bridal bouquets should be anything but bland. This gorgeous arrangement pairs show-stopping succulents with wildflowers and baby's breath to create a truly unique bouquet. This bouquet also includes white flowers, giving the arrangement a softer and more feminine look and adding contrast to the bright colors of the succulents.

As a bonus, these instructions cover both a bride's bouquet as well as one for a bridesmaid. In addition to an array of succulents in pinks, purples, and blues, this bouquet features Ursula Purple Thistle and Silver Dollar Eucalyptus, both of which have a longer shelf life than many other cut flowers.

MATERIALS NEEDED

- 22-gauge floral wire
- Thick floral picks
- Floral tape
- Ribbon or twine
- Hot glue gun
- Bride bouquet: 5 faux flowers (I used Sola Wood Flowers)

SUCCULENTS AND PLANTS USED (FOR BRIDE)

- Seven 4" (10cm) succulent rosettes:
  - *Echeveria* 'Perle von Nurnberg'
  - *Aeonium* 'Kiwi'
  - *Echeveria* 'Blue Rose'
  - *Echeveria* 'Melaco'
- Ten 2" (5cm) succulent rosettes
- *Senecio rowleyanus*
- Baby's breath
- *Oligoneuron rigidum*
- Various greenery clippings, including Jasmine leaves, Eucalyptus, and Limonium

SUCCULENTS AND PLANTS USED (FOR BRIDESMAID)

- Three 4" (10cm) Echeveria rosettes:
  - *Echeveria* 'Curly Locks'
  - *Echeveria* 'Blue Rose'
  - *Echeveria* 'Gold Light'
- Seven 2" (5cm) succulent rosettes
- Silver Dollar Eucalyptus
- Baby's breath
- Ursula Purple Thistle

Bridesmaid

Make this bouquet your own by pairing succulents with flowers found in your area. The one shown was inspired by local California flora of succulents, desert flowers, and beautiful greenery.

Bridesmaid

Bride

1. Prepare the succulents. Remove any soil from rooted plants by gently massaging away the dirt.

Bridesmaid

Bride

Bridesmaid

Bride

2. Create the smaller succulent stems. Cut 24" (61cm) of floral wire using wire cutters. Pierce the stem or the stub at the base of the succulent plant and bring the wire through to the other side. Pull the wire until the ends are even and in a U shape, facing downward. Gently twist the wires together to form a stem. Repeat with any succulents that have a stem less than 1" (2.5cm) long.

3. Wrap each stem with floral tape. Gently pull the floral tape to activate its "stickiness." Start at the top of the stem by the base of the succulents. Wrap the floral tape in a slanted spiral downward until you reach the base of the stem. Use your fingers to pinch the tape as you go to help it stick to itself.

Bride

Bride

Bride

4. Create the larger succulent stems. Using a thick floral pick will create sturdier stems. Pierce the succulent's stem with the stick, then wrap it in floral tape.

5. Bride bouquet: Create the faux flower stems. Place some hot glue on the underside of the flower. Insert a floral pick.

6. Prep the other flowers and greenery. Trim the stems to match the length of the wired succulents. Strip off any leaves on the bottom stem portions of the plants.

Bridesmaid

Bride

Bridesmaid

Bride

7. Experiment with the arrangement of flowers and succulents. Hold them as close to the base as possible as you arrange them together. Keep the larger succulents toward the center of the bouquet. Filler plants, such as the baby's breath, should go around the back and sides to add volume. Bride bouquet: Disperse the smaller succulents and sola wood flowers around the center of the bouquet. Bridesmaid bouquet: Disperse the smaller succulents and purple thistle around the center of the bouquet.

8. Hold the plants tightly and tie everything together with a piece of twine. Because succulents are much heavier than traditional flowers, this step will make it easier to add leaves and additional filler flowers without the center of the arrangement falling apart.

Bride

Bridesmaid

Bride

9. Trim the stems to the same length. Since most of the stems are made from wire, use the wire cutter.

10. Wrap the stems together with floral tape. Gently pull the floral tape to activate its "stickiness," and wrap it tightly back on itself as you go.

Bridesmaid

Bride

Bride

11. Decide if you are finished or want to add more. If you want a more minimalistic bouquet, or something smaller for a bridesmaid, you can skip to step 15 to finish the bouquet.

12. Add greenery and filler flowers to make the bouquet voluminous. You can also add on more small succulents to your liking.

Bride

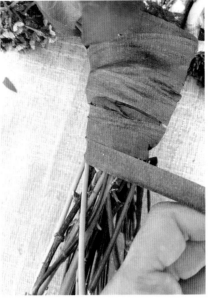

Bride

13. Tie everything off with twine. Trim stems to the same length. Wrap the stems with floral tape, starting near the base of the plants.

14. If desired, add trailing succulents to the bouquet. Strip off about 3" (7.5cm) of leaves near the root of the succulents. Secure the base of the trailing succulents to the front and center of the bouquet using floral tape.

Bridesmaid

Bride

15. Finish the bouquet with ribbon. Apply a spot of hot glue to the top of the wrapped stems, on the back of the arrangement. Press the cut end of the ribbon onto the hot glue, being careful not to burn your fingers. Tightly wrap the ribbon by spiraling it downward until all the floral tape is covered. Cut the ribbon with enough room to fold it back on itself, and glue it to the back of the bouquet. Apply another small spot of glue to secure the ribbon and finish your gorgeous bouquet!

CARE

Succulent bouquets can be made a few days before your event. The cut flowers and leaves used in this project will also last for about two days. If you add any more delicate cut flowers, such as roses or peonies, to the bouquet, it will need to be made the day of the event. When you are finished with your bouquet, plant the succulents by carefully removing the plants from the floral tape and wire, then placing them in well-draining soil.

LIGHTED MOON TOPIARY

 Intermediate

Blue and white colored succulents were used to create a lunar look using a moss sphere. To make it even more magical (especially in the dark), the moon is wrapped in cool white fairy lights. Moss balls can be purchased in a variety of sizes, with or without hanging hardware attached. Your sphere can also be displayed on a table by leaving the bottom half unplanted and placing it in a wide-mouthed vase.

MATERIALS NEEDED

- 6"–7" (15–18cm) premade moss ball, hanging hardware attached
- Scissors
- Floral pins
- Screwdriver or pencil
- Hot glue gun
- Bowl of water
- 20 ft. (6m) battery-operated LED fairy lights

SUCCULENTS USED

- Seventy-five 2" (5cm) succulents:
  - ×*Graptoveria* 'Moonglow'
  - *Sedum clavatum*
  - *Echeveria setosa*
  - *Sedum pachyphyllum*
- Several small filler plants in the same varieties

Moss spheres make a wonderful decoration for any event and can be made in the colors that match other decor. For example, use greens and reds for Christmas or orange-hued succulents for an autumn-inspired creation.

1. Gather and prepare the succulents. Remove soil and leaves from around the base so you have a clean stem.

2. Soak moss topiary in a large bucket of water for about 30 minutes until it is completely saturated. Moss is messy and holds a lot of water, so cover the work surface with a large towel before beginning.

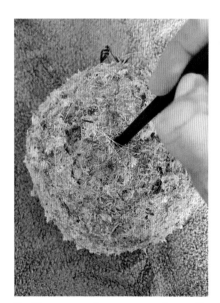

3. Prepare the moss sphere for planting. Use a pointy tool, such as a pencil or screwdriver, to make the first hole where you want to place the succulent stem. Place a spot of hot glue in the hole you made. Put the stem of the succulent in the hole to secure it in place.

4. If needed, use a floral pin to hold the succulent in place. This is recommended for larger succulents or ones that do not have a very long stem. Simply pierce the stem at the base and then press the pin into the moss.

5. Keep repeating this process until half of the moon is planted.

6. Hang the moon to complete the opposite side. This will prevent crushing the succulents. Once the moon is complete, take a step back and add smaller filler plants anywhere that it is needed.

7. To add lights, wrap the LED light strand around the circumference of the moon. Start at the top and wrap down and back up. Secure the LED battery to the top of the moon using floral pins, trying to conceal it under the leaves of the larger succulents. Display your living succulent moon by hanging it from the ceiling.

CARE

Place in an area that receives bright, indirect sunlight. Water when moss is completely dried out, which is about once per week depending on the humidity of your area. To water, submerge in water for five minutes. You can use a water-soluble fertilizer every 1–2 months to help keep the plants healthy. When succulents begin to grow out of the arrangement after about 6–8 months, you can gently remove them and plant them in soil. Your topiary form can be replanted with fresh plants.

LIGHTED STAR TOPIARY

 Intermediate

This stunning living succulent topiary can be made separately or together with the Lighted Moon. LED fairy lights bring a little extra magic to this unique décor, making a perfect nighttime decoration for your event or patio. A simple pattern creates visual interest and showcases several varieties of colorful succulents. Feel free to follow this pattern or create your own unique rainbow using the plants you have on hand.

MATERIALS NEEDED

- 16" (40.5cm) premade moss star, hanging hardware attached
- Scissors
- Bucket of water
- Floral pins
- Screwdriver or pencil
- Hot glue gun
- 33 ft. (10m) battery-operated LED fairy lights

SUCCULENTS USED

- Points of the star:
  - *Aeonium* 'Kiwi,' in various sizes
  - *Graptopetalum paraguayense*
  - *×Graptosedum* 'Vera Higgins'
  - *Sedum clavatum*
  - *Sedum adolphi*
- Around the center:
  - *Crassula ovata*
  - *Echeveria harmsii* 'Ruby Slippers'
  - *Sedum xrubrotinctum*
  - *Sedeveria* 'Sorrento'
- Center of star:
  - 4" (10cm) *×Graptoveria* 'Opalina'

Note: The succulents in the star points were purchased in 4" (10cm) pots with about five succulents per pot. You will need two of these 4" (10cm) containers for each variety. The Jade and other varieties around the large Opalina were cuttings taken from larger plants in 8" (20cm) buckets.

You could use blue, white, and gray succulents to match the Lighted Moon project. Another idea would be to create a 4th of July theme using coordinating red, white, and blue succulents and lights.

1. Prepare the succulents by removing all soil. Succulent cuttings should sit for 1–2 days prior to placing in the wet moss. The stems should be between ½"–1" (1–2.5cm) with leaves carefully removed. If your succulent does not have a stem, it will be secured with a floral pin. Soak moss topiary in a large bucket of water for an hour before planting it. Moss is messy and holds a lot of water, so I recommend covering your work surface with a large towel before beginning.

2. Practice arranging the succulents on the star. For the design shown, use larger succulents at the base and make them progressively smaller as you move toward the point. Choose a large succulent as the focal point emphasize it with the *Crassula ovata* and *Echeveria* angled outward, toward the star points. Brightly colored red *Sedum* emphasizes the center of each point.

3. Prepare the moss star for planting. Use a pointy tool, such as a pencil or screwdriver, to make the first hole in the moss in which to place the succulent.

4. Place a spot of hot glue in the hole you made. Put the stem of the succulent in the opening to secure it to the star. You can also use floral pins instead of hot glue to secure the succulents. Keep repeating this process to fill the star.

5. Occasionally take a step back to look at the arrangement. Add smaller plants in between larger succulents to fill up gaps and make everything symmetrical. If any hot glue dripped down the sides of the star, wait until it dries, then remove it with your fingers or gently cut it off with scissors.

6. Wrap the lights around the circumference of the star 3–4 times. Start near the top of the sides, closer to the succulents. With a floral pin, secure one end of the lights to the moss in the corner of any side. Wrap outward to the star point and back to the other corner. Secure the light stand with a floral pin. Keep repeating, securing the lights in each corner. Create two more lines of lights, 1" (2.5cm) and 2" (5cm) below the first. If you have more of the light strand remaining, continue to wrap the star until you run out.

7. Secure the LED battery to the back of the star. Hang your star on a wall or prop up on a table to be displayed.

CARE

Place in an area that receives bright, indirect sunlight. Water when moss is completely dried out, which is about once per week depending on the humidity of your area. To water, submerge in water for five minutes. You can use a water-soluble fertilizer every 1–2 months to help keep the plants healthy. When succulents begin to grow out of the arrangement after about 6–8 months, you can gently remove them and plant them in soil. Your topiary form can be replanted with fresh plants.

LIVING SUCCULENT FLOWER CROWN

 Intermediate

Stand out from the crowd with a gorgeous living succulent flower crown. Unlike regular flowers, which can die quickly, a crown adorned with succulents can last weeks. These are so much fun to make and perfect for children and adults alike. Crowns can be one-size-fits-all when fashioned with a ribbon, as shown. If you prefer, you can also take a head measurement and make the crown to size with succulents around the whole diameter.

MATERIALS NEEDED

- 22-gauge floral wire
- Grapevine wire
- Floral tape
- Ribbon or twine

SUCCULENTS AND PLANTS USED

- Eleven 2" (5cm) succulent rosettes:
  - *Echeveria* 'Tippy'
  - 3 *Echeveria harmsii* 'Ruby Slippers'
  - *Sempervivum arachnoideum*
  - ×*Graptoveria* 'Bashful'
  - *Echeveria* 'Blue Rose'
  - 3 *Graptopetalum paraguayense*
  - *Sempervivum* 'Ohio Burgandy'
- 1 small ×*Graptosedum* 'Vera Higgins'
- 4 small cuttings of baby's breath

Flower crowns make the perfect
wedding accessory for flower girls,
bridesmaids, and brides. Or create one
for a fun event like a fairy tea party!

2. Cut 17" (43cm) of grapevine wire. Create small loops at either end of the wire by bending it back on itself.

3. Wrap the wire in floral tape starting at the base of one loop. Gently pull the floral tape to activate its "stickiness." Wrap the tape around the loop you created several times to secure it. Continue along the rest of the wire until you reach the opposite loop.

1. Remove any soil from the succulent roots. The crown shown uses mostly succulents with just a little bit of baby's breath at the ends of the crown. You can optionally add other leaves, such as eucalyptus, to give it a fuller look.

4. Bend the wire into a crown shape using your hands.

5. Arrange the succulents around the crown until you find a design you like. Start by placing larger succulents toward the center and fill up the rest of the crown with filler plants. Place them to the side in the same layout or take a photo.

6. Create the succulent stems.
Cut 4" (10cm) of floral wire using wire cutters. Pierce the stem or the stub at the base of the succulent plant and bring the wire through to the other side. Pull the wire until the ends are even and in a U shape, facing downward. Gently twist the wires together to form a stem. Repeat with any succulents that have a stem less than 1" (2.5cm) long.

7. Assemble the wired succulents on the crown.
Place one at a time by wrapping the stem you created around the base. Begin with the larger succulents at the center of the crown and go outward to each side.

8. Assemble the natural stem succulents on the crown.
Secure them to the crown using floral tape. Use floral tape around the wrapped wire stems to further secure the succulents.

9. Add ribbon through the loops. Place the crown onto your head and adjust to a comfortable size. Secure it by pulling the ribbons into a bow.

CARE

Your succulent crown should last about a week. Very carefully remove the plants by unwrapping the floral tape and wire. Your succulents can then be planted in soil. Succulent stem cuttings will grow roots after a week or so.

LIVING SUCCULENT MIRROR FRAME

 Intermediate–Advanced

This magical succulent mirror reminds me of something you might find in a secret garden, hidden among the flowers, as an unexpected intrigue. Some English gardens have mirrors to create an optical illusion that the space is larger. This mirror is perfect to place in a shaded spot of your yard, patio, or garden that receives bright, indirect sunlight. You can also position your mirror to capture light and brighten shady spots.

This craft looks very impressive when finished but it's actually quite simple to create. Even the novice crafter can shape chicken wire and use a staple gun to attach it to the wood. This project uses *a lot* of succulents, so use every cutting from your collection you have on hand.

MATERIALS NEEDED

- 39" x 25" (99 x 63.5cm) mirror with 5" x 25" x 2" (13 x 63.5 x 5cm) wooden frame
- 1 lb. (450g) bale sphagnum moss
- Green forest moss and reindeer moss in various colors
- Chicken wire
- Wire cutters
- Work gloves
- Staple gun
- Hot glue gun
- Floral pins

Note: The mirror used for this project was found at a thrift store. If your mirror does not have a bottom ledge, you can follow just the instructions for planting the sides. You could also only plant the top of the mirror.

SUCCULENTS USED

- Eleven 4" (10cm) succulent rosettes
- Thirty 2" (5cm) succulent rosettes
- Blooming succulents:
  - *Calandrinia grandiflora*
- Variety of small filler succulents
- Some of the varieties used included:
  - *Aeonium* 'Kiwi'
  - *Echeveria* 'Hawaii'
  - *Graptopetalum* 'Superbum'
  - ×*Graptoveria* 'Opalina'
  - *Echeveria* 'Melaco'
  - *Echeveria* 'Blue Bird'
  - *Echeveria* 'Blue Prince'
  - *Echeveria* 'Minima'
  - *Crassula pellucida* subsp. *marginalis*
  - *Crassula ovata* 'Gollum Jade'
  - *Echeveria* 'Neon Breaker'
  - ×*Graptoveria* 'Debbie'
  - *Sedum* ×*rubrotinctum*
  - ×*Graptosedum* 'Francesco Baldi'
  - ×*Graptosedum* 'Vera Higgins'
  - *Crassula ovata* 'Dwarf Jade Plant'
  - *Crassula ovata* 'Curly Jade'
  - *Echeveria* 'Blue Atoll'
  - *Echeveria* 'Red Fireball'

This mirror will truly transform your garden into a living work of art, creating an unexpected dimension. Use as many colorful and blooming succulents you can get your hands on for this project.

1. Find a mirror with a shelf or build a shelf to attach to the mirror. You could create something similar with a smaller frame, but try to find a mirror with a 2"–3" (5–7.5cm) rim to build the moss bed on top of. Disclaimer: This project is messy and will get wet moss everywhere! Set your worktable outside or cover the surface with a tablecloth.

2. Soak the sphagnum moss in water for 10 minutes.

3. Line the sides of the mirror with the moss. Place the mirror on its back on a flat surface. Squeeze out excess water and place it along the sides of the frame. Pack it tightly in an oblong shape as if you are creating a loaf. Create as thick of a moss base as you can in which to plant the succulents.

 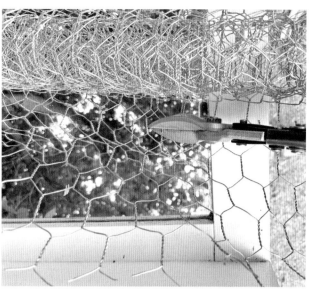

4. Measure the length of the moss-lined mirror. Cut the chicken wire so it covers the length of the sides and will wrap around the entire moss section. Make sure the wire fits over the moss tightly. I cut a 5" (13cm) wide strip to place it on top. Remember to put on your work gloves to avoid cutting your hands and fingers.

5. Use the hands to mold the chicken wire on top of the moss. Press down on the outside edges to create a tight mold to staple down.

6. With the staple gun, secure the moss and wire to the frame of the mirror. Starting on the outside edges, place a staple on every 1" (2.5cm) section of chicken wire to hold it in place. Continue on the inside edges, being mindful not to break the mirror.

7. Cut off excess wire with the cutters. Be careful to collect these little wire bits when you are done so you don't step on them. They're very sharp!

8. Use hot glue to add a bit of green moss to the outside and inside edges of the mirror. This adds more color and hides any staples. Move the mirror from lying flat to propped up. You now have most of the moss frame completed!

9. Place moss on the bottom of the mirror as you did in the previous steps. The shelf provides the room to create a thicker layer of moss to plant more succulents in.

10. Measure the area and cut the chicken wire to size. Mold the wire onto the moss frame. Staple the wire to the outer edge of the frame and trim off any excess. Fold the inner part of the wire firmly into and around the shape of the moss, away from the mirror. Do not staple the inner part as you did with the sides of the mirror. Fold the wire on the outer edges in toward the frame to keep the moss in place.

11. Fill in the bottom, outer edge of the mirror. Lay the mirror flat on your worktable. With the hot glue gun, secure green reindeer moss to the bottom part of the moss-and-wire base to hide the staples. Start planting with filler plants, such as *Crassula ovata*, and small succulent rosettes. If needed, use a little hot glue to help the plants stay in place. This does not hurt the plant at all.

12. Plant the sides of the mirror. If the moss has dried out, add a little water using a pitcher. This will make it more pliable for planting. Work in large batches by using a flat of 2" (5cm) succulents. Remove the succulent from its container and gently massage off all the dirt. Make a small space in the moss by using your finger or a pointy tool, then place the roots there. Use a floral pin or hot glue the secure the succulent to the frame. Continue planting until both sides of the mirror are covered with succulents.

13. Optional: Secure green moss. Use hot glue on the outer edges of the mirror sides to give it a more finished look. This also covers up any staples.

14. Add filler plants around the rosettes. As you did before, use floral pins or hot glue to hold these smaller plants in place. You can also add little bits of green moss to the inside edges or on any bare spots.

15. Prop the mirror against a wall to plant on the shelf. The thicker moss base is perfect for the bigger plants to flourish and grow. As you make holes to plant the succulents, you can optionally add a little bit of soil for the plants. If the plants' roots are too big to fit through the chicken wire, use cutters to make the hole slightly bigger. Use floral pins to better secure the plants to the moss.

16. Use taller succulent and blooming succulents along the back edge. This adds layers to the arrangement. I used blooming *Calandrinia grandiflora* on the right side of the mirror to create a beautiful visual.

17. Layer moss from the top down the sides so it looks as if it is growing naturally. Use hot glue to secure the moss. If desired, plant extra succulents so they wrap from the front to the side to achieve a more organic effect.

18. Top the mirror off with moss to give it a softer, more magical look. Use hot glue on the wood and then carefully attach the moss. Layer different kinds of moss and add natural elements, such as bark, for a rustic look.

CARE

Water the succulents about once a week using a watering can with a directed spray. Make sure the moss is completely dried out between watering. The succulents will grow roots into the moss. Once the plants outgrow their home, you can transplant them into your garden or into another container with soil.

VERTICAL GARDEN WALL HANGING

 **Advanced**

To give your indoor or outdoor décor an unexpected boost, display this magical arrangement that is beautiful enough to adorn a gallery! Keep it simple by just using succulents or up the ante with crystals, colorful moss, and shells. I wanted this project to be reminiscent of a painting, something interesting to study and enjoy. Instead of canvas and paints, our medium is colorful moss, living succulents, and silk butterflies.

This vertical wall hanging is made from a repurposed wine box found on the side of the road. Wine boxes can be readily found at your local wine shop, winery, or even restaurant. With a little plastic liner to protect the wood from water damage, your planter will last for years to come.

MATERIALS NEEDED

- 23" x 13½" x 5" (58.5 x 34 x 13cm) wine box
- Optional: Wood stain
- Optional: Paintbrush
- Plastic liner
- French cleat hanger
- Staple gun and staples
- Pencil
- Electric drill
- Small screws
- Perlite
- Well-draining succulent & cactus soil
- Optional: Fertilizer pellets
- Mountain moss
- Green forest moss and reindeer moss in various colors
- Chicken wire
- Wire cutters
- Work gloves
- Hot glue gun
- Extra décor: Crystals, shells, driftwood, dried Limonium, butterflies, etc.
- Floral wire
- Optional: Battery-operated LED fairy lights

SUCCULENTS AND PLANTS USED

- 4" (10cm) succulents:
  - *Aeonium* 'Kiwi'
  - *Echeveria* 'Blue Atoll'
  - *×Graptoveria* 'Opalina'
  - *Echeveria* 'Perle von Nurnberg'
  - *Echeveria* 'Emerald Ripple'
  - *Aeonium* 'Sunburst'
  - *Echeveria* 'Dusty Rose'
- 2" (5cm) succulents and cuttings:
  - *Aeonium* 'Kiwi'
  - *Echeveria* 'Hawaii'
  - *Graptopetalum paraguayense*
  - *Graptopetalum* 'Superbum'
  - *×Graptosedum* 'Vera Higgins'
  - *×Graptoveria* 'Opalina'
  - *Echeveria* 'Melaco'
  - *Echeveria agavoides*
  - *Kalanchoe tubiflora*
  - *Curio radicans*
  - *Echeveria* 'Blue Bird'
  - *Echeveria* 'Blue Prince'
  - *Echeveria* 'Minima'
  - *Crassula pellucida* subsp. *marginalis*
  - *Crassula ovata* 'Gollum Jade'
  - *Echeveria* 'Neon Breaker'
  - *×Graptoveria* 'Debbie'

  Note: About 40 total succulents in different sizes were used.

- *Portulaca* 'ColorBlast Plumberry'

  Note: This is not a succulent, but it tolerates the same conditions of heat, drought, and sun.

Your box can be hung, propped up on a table, or put against a wall. Display your creation at a dinner party with fine wine bottles displayed next to it or add more LED lights to create a nighttime spectacle.

1. Optional: Stain the wine box. Clean off any debris by hosing it down or wiping it with a wet cloth. Paint the outside and sides of the wine box using wood stain. You can paint the inside of the box, but since it will be covered by plants, it is not necessary. Be aware of paint dripping down the sides; wipe it off or brush it out to have an even finish. Let the paint on the wine box dry before moving on to the next step.

2. Fill the wine box with a plastic liner. This will protect it from water damage. Cut the liner to the dimensions of the box interior and staple it in. Use a staple every 3" (7.5cm) to hold it in place.

3. Attach a French cleat hanger to the back. This tool is necessary if you're hanging the piece since it is heavy. Measure the length of the wine box and place the hanger halfway; in this case, it is 11½" (29cm). Use a pencil to mark the placement.

4. Measure the French cleat hanger and mark its middle point. Position the hanger so the middle part matches the marked middle of the wine box. Use an electric drill to secure the hanger to the box in two places.

5. Confirm the bottom of the hanger fits. When you hang the vertical garden, the opposite hanger will fit under the piece you just attached, as shown. This piece will be screwed into the wall.

6. Fill the box with perlite to ¼ full. This will help absorb excess moisture when you water the arrangement.

7. Pack the box with soil. Fill it all the way to the top. Pat it down and add more because the soil will settle. Optional but awesome: Add fertilizer pellets to help your plants thrive.

8. Cover the soil with a small layer of mountain moss. This will help the plants and soil remain intact when hung.

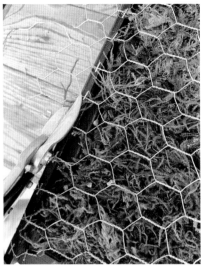

9. Measure the chicken wire so it covers the base of the box. Position the uncut side onto the long side of the box. Press it down so it lays flat. This will secure everything in place. You can also use smaller hardware cloth, but it would have to be cut when planting larger root stems. Wear gloves when handling chicken wire.

10. Cut the chicken wire. Cut it close so the wire isn't sticking out of the edges but long enough to have wire to adhere to the side of the box. Staple the wire to the frame. Place a staple every 1" (2.5cm) to secure it in place.

11. Cut off any excess wire sticking out.

12. Make a moss frame to cover the chicken wire. Use hot glue to adhere different colors of moss around the edges. This gives the box a more finished look.

13. Add decorations on top of the moss frame. You can add shells, driftwood, crystals, etc., to make it your own.

14. Arrange the succulents and clippings on the moss "canvas." Prepare the plants by stripping off the leaves at the base so you have 2" (5cm) to plant into the soil.

15. This arrangement uses two *Curio radicans* to create an interesting line across. Secure the whole thing using floral pins angled underneath the chicken wire. Wrap floral wire around the stem and the chicken wire. Or use a floral pin every 4" (10cm) to secure it in place. The trailing succulents will grow roots along the entire length to attach to the moss.

16. Optional: Tuck LED fairy lights close to the *Curio radicans*. String them along the *C. radicans*, tuck the line under the leaves, and secure with the floral pins that are already there. Hide the base of the lights under a plant in the arrangement. Make sure the on/off switch is facing up for easy access.

18. Continue planting and arranging. Occasionally take a step back to view your art and fill in any bare spots with smaller succulents or moss.

17. Attach the succulents to the frame. Use a pointy tool or your finger to make a space in the moss, then insert the root of the succulent. If the succulent does not have a stem or root, use hot glue to secure it in place. For larger succulents with a longer stem, plant them in the soil; you may need to use a floral pin to secure them in place.

19. Create the butterfly section in the center. Glue colorful moss where you are going to place them. They will go over the moss to make them stand out. Attach each butterfly using a small spot of hot glue. They also come on very thin metal wire which is inserted into the soil.

20. Insert crystals. Ideally, find stones that will fit snuggly into the chicken wire. If needed, use a little hot glue before inserting. The crystal used here is a natural citrine, a stone said to attract abundance.

21. Create conch shell planted with succulent. Place a little hot glue in the shell, add moss, and glue the mini succulent cuttings into the moss. The cuttings will eventually grow small roots into the shell. When they outgrow it, you can plant them in a pot and leave the shell as is or place new plants inside of it. After planting, attach the shell to the base using hot glue.

CARE

Water every week or when soil and moss feel completely dried out. Be mindful not to overwater as the planter does not have drainage holes! When watering, remove the box from the wall and lay it flat. Be sure to water in the early evening, never the middle of the day, because succulents can get root rot or get sunburned from water droplets on their leaves. When the plants eventually outgrow the planter, you can transplant them into another pot.

22. Place dried purple Limonium. It complements the small amethyst tree next to it. The dried flower stems are inserted in the soil and the tree is secured using a spot of glue.

23. Let the arrangement sit flat for 3–4 weeks before hanging. If you want to display it in that time, you could prop it up on a table or against a wall with a slight tilt. This way of displaying also gives a nice three-dimensional look while showing off the wine box. Once the succulents have had a chance to root into the soil, you can hang it.

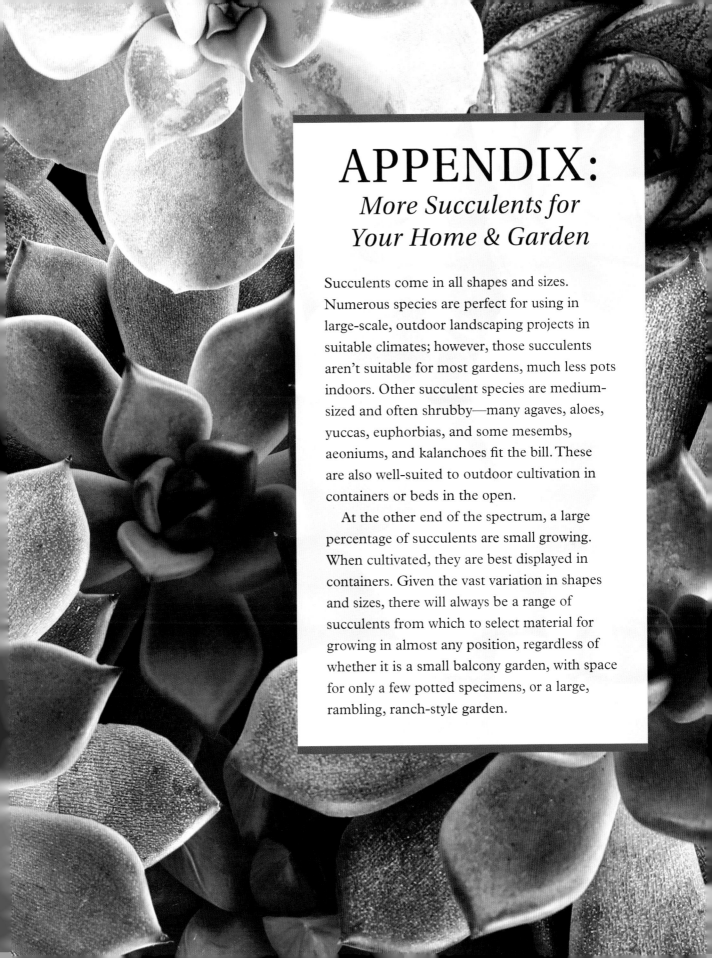

APPENDIX:
More Succulents for Your Home & Garden

Succulents come in all shapes and sizes. Numerous species are perfect for using in large-scale, outdoor landscaping projects in suitable climates; however, those succulents aren't suitable for most gardens, much less pots indoors. Other succulent species are medium-sized and often shrubby—many agaves, aloes, yuccas, euphorbias, and some mesembs, aeoniums, and kalanchoes fit the bill. These are also well-suited to outdoor cultivation in containers or beds in the open.

At the other end of the spectrum, a large percentage of succulents are small growing. When cultivated, they are best displayed in containers. Given the vast variation in shapes and sizes, there will always be a range of succulents from which to select material for growing in almost any position, regardless of whether it is a small balcony garden, with space for only a few potted specimens, or a large, rambling, ranch-style garden.

Agave pygmaea

AGAVACEAE

Representatives of the Agavaceae are mostly leaf succulents that have their leaves arranged in strong rosettes. Species of *Agave* are generally known as century plants. This is an allusion to the fact that they generally take many years, in rare cases 15 to 20 or more, to reach flowering maturity.

Most species of *Agave* are very easy to cultivate and make excellent companions for cacti. As a general rule, agaves are monocarpic. This means that they grow for many years and then flower once before dying.

Apart from producing copious amounts of seed, many agaves also produce bulbils (perfectly formed plantlets) on their inflorescences. These root easily and can be planted to ensure the next generation of that species in a garden.

Most species of the family are remarkably hardy and will easily survive in dry, cold winter conditions. Under colder climatic conditions, *Agave* should be protected from growing in anything that becomes waterlogged in winter. Species originating from tropical areas such as the Caribbean islands will, however, show varying degrees of leaf damage at temperatures below 32°F (0°C).

Representatives of a number of other agavoid genera are common in cultivation in many parts of the world. Some of these are discussed here.

Like so many cacti, they also originate from the western hemisphere, particularly Mexico and the southern USA. Some species, for example *Agave americana* and *Agave sisalana*, sucker excessively and care should be taken that they are not planted too close to prized cacti as they will very rapidly smother them.

It has been suggested that the Agavaceae should be included in the Asparagaceae, but we here retain it as a family in its own right.

Agave attenuata

The soft leaved *Agave attenuata* is perfect for cultivaton in subtropical areas with a mild climate.

Plants grow as medium-sized shrubs to small single-trunked trees that carry large rosettes at the ends of the stems. The leaves are very soft and pliable, in contrast to those of most species of *Agave*. The leaf margins and both leaf surfaces are smooth and devoid of any spines. The leaves stiffen and twirl as they dry and are easily shed, exposing a smooth, clean stem.

The inflorescence grows vertically at first, after which it gracefully curves outward in the shape of the trunk of an elephant. The large flowers are a light green color.

The species hails from Mexico, but is now found all over the world. It is a wonderful landscape plant for tropical and subtropical gardens, but the leaves are easily damaged by harsh climates and subzero temperatures.

Agave desmetiana

Agave desmetiana is exceedingly hardy in dry conditions. It is widely cultivated in desert areas. Pictured is *Agave desmetiana* 'Variegata' that has yellow leaf margins.

This must be one of the easiest agaves for garden cultivation. In addition, it includes a number of very desirable forms—ranging from a variously very light green, almost white one, known as *A. desmetiana* 'Joe Hoak,' through the regular, dark green colored one, to a yellow-leaf-margined form—that are available in the horticultural trade.

The species also shows some variation in leaf armature, with some being almost smooth-margined, while others have scattered teeth on the margins. Inflorescences are fairly short and carry yellow flowers on squat-looking side branches. After having flowered, a profusion of bulbils develop on the inflorescence. These can be easily removed and planted. Plants will also slowly pup from the base to yield medium-sized stands. They will grow very well and flower in medium-sized to large containers.

Agave filifera

The leaf margins of *Agave filifera* are adorned with threadlike appendages (left). A plant of Mexican origin, *Agave filifera* has striking purple flowers (right). It can withstand a wide range of temperatures.

Plants grow as medium-sized rosettes that sucker prolifically from the base. The leaves are light green and sharply tipped. Both leaf surfaces are adorned with longitudinal white bands and marginal threads haphazardly curl away from the leaf margins.

A tall, unbranched inflorescence is produced after many years. Large, purplish green flowers are carried on short stalks along the upper two thirds of an inflorescence.

A useful agave for landscaping, as it takes up to 18 years to reach flowering age, while it slowly increases in size to form large clumps of more or less ball-shaped rosettes. Propagation is almost exclusively from the side shoots it produces.

Agave geminiflora

The leaves of *Agave geminiflora* are thin and pliable and adorned with white marginal threads.

Plants grow as single, unbranched, medium-sized rosettes. The leaves are bright green, fairly thin, and pliable and their margins are beautifully adorned with short, white threads. (The leaves of some forms lack the white threads, but the most desirable ones to grow are those with prominent marginal threads.) The set of young leaves in the center of a rosette are tightly packed into a compact cone.

After many years of growth, a single, unbranched flowering pole is produced. The flowers, borne in small clusters, are greenish, tinged with red.

This noninvasive Mexican species does not form plantlets from the base. Propagation is through seed that germinates easily.

ABOUT AGAVES

Species of the horticulturally useful genus *Agave* are generally referred to as century plants because they take many years to flower—but certainly not a hundred years! Even the most long-lived of the agaves will flower more or less within 15–20 years. Once they have flowered, they die, leaving seed that will rapidly germinate, or they sprout plantlets, either at the base of the plant or on the inflorescence. The plants formed in the latter way are called bulbils and are perfect miniatures of the mature mother plant.

Agave guadalajarana

The leaf margins of *Agave guadalajarana* are adorned with striking, reddish brown teeth. Inset photo. The flowers of *Agave guadalajarana* are light green and carry contrasting reddish purple filaments, while the anthers are yellow.

This is a medium-sized species that will easily grow and ultimately even flower in a plant container with a diameter of 14" (35cm). The leaves are armed with short, sharp teeth that are carried on small protrusions or teats. Leaf tips are further adorned with very sharp tips. The teeth themselves are reddish brown and contrast with the bluish green leaf surface, which is slightly rough to the touch.

The inflorescence is branched and carries light green, vertically disposed flowers on the side branches. The filaments are prominently purplish red, contrasting with the green flowers. This species is very resistant to virtually all pests that will attack agaves. Plants remain solitary and must be reproduced from seed.

Agave lophantha 'Quadricolor'

The horticultural selection known as *Agave lophantha* 'Quadricolor' has strikingly colored leaves with bright yellow longitudinal sections that contrast against shades of green.

Plants are many-leaved and grow into medium-sized specimens that sprout a multitude of pups from the base. The leaves vary in color from yellowish green to dark green with an even lighter green, longitudinal midsection running along the length of the leaf. The leaf margins are armed with very sharp, often grayish teeth. After many years of growth—as much as 15, or even more—a plant will produce an inflorescence of about 12 ft. (3.5m) tall.

Flowers are bright greenish yellow. Plants can be easily multiplied by removing and rooting the plantlets that develop from the base. The ideal spot to keep the plant is in full sun or in bright, dappled shade.

Agave mitis

Agave mitis is proliferous. If planted against a slope, its blue rosettes resemble a cascading waterfall.

Plants grow as robust, multiheaded shrubs, with medium-sized rosettes tightly packed in a clump. The leaves are light green to bluish white, and the margins have small, brown teeth.

After six to eight years, a robust, unbranched inflorescence appears from the center of a rosette. The flowers are fairly large and green, tinged with red. The tips of the floral segments are strongly recurved, giving the inflorescence an almost fluffy appearance.

When clumps of this Mexican species mature, it seems that, at any time, at least one rosette is producing an inflorescence. (Only the rosette that produces an inflorescence dies. The rest of the clump keeps growing.)

The best horticultural feature is the neat, open rosettes that in time form dense strands. Their clumping habit means that once a rosette has flowered and starts to wither, it is rapidly replaced by another, so that gaps do not develop in the greenery.

The form of *Agave mitis*, sometimes referred to as *A. mitis* var. *albidior*, illustrated here, has bluish gray leaves. Forms with bright green or greenish gray leaves are also common in cultivation. However, the form illustrated here is the most striking.

Agave nizandensis

A small rosette of *Agave nizandensis*. At first sight the species looks like a miniature aloe rather than like an agave. Inset photo. The inflorescences of *Agave nizandensis* are sparsely branched and few-flowered.

Most agaves grow as medium-sized to very large specimens that in time usually develop formidable rosettes with the leaves additionally armed with sharp spines that are sure to cause pain if unsuspecting passerby bumps into them. Not many agaves remain small and manageable as pot plants. However, *Agave nizandensis* is a notable exception. It is one of the few agaves that will happily grow and thrive, even flower, in a small pot, for example when kept on a sunny windowsill.

Leaves are also un-agave-like, being quite brittle. The upper leaf surface often carries a prominent lighter yellowish green midsection. The thin inflorescence branches higher up and carries clusters of large, greenish flowers in an erect position.

Agave ornithobroma

The leaves of *Agave ornithobroma* are adorned with white, curly threads.

A selection of species of agave has leaves that are adorned with threads along their margins. In very few species is this character better developed than in *Agave ornithobroma*. The threadlike filaments slowly peel away from the leaf margins to give the rosette of the species a distinctly cobweb-like appearance. The leaves are quite long—usually longer than in the similar-looking *Agave geminiflora*—and tend to be gracefully recurved, like a water fountain. The inflorescence is an unbranched spike and the species clumps from the base. These basal sprouts can be removed and grown on.

Agave pygmaea

The reddish brown spine at the tip of a leaf of *Agave pygmaea* is very sharp and contrasts with the dull light green leaf surface. Inset photo. *Agave pygmaea* carries dense clusters of bright yellow flowers on the short side branches of an inflorescence.

Plants grow as solitary, medium-sized to large, ball-shaped rosettes. The dull, light green leaves are somewhat sandpapery and carry small, dark reddish brown teeth on the margins. Leaves are sword-shaped, narrowing toward the base, broadening in the middle, and tapering toward the tip. The terminal spine on a leaf is very sharp, prominent, and reddish brown.

The inflorescence is branched and carries bright yellow flowers erectly on the side branches. Plants do not sprout from the base and do not develop plantlets on the inflorescence. Multiplication is through seed.

Agave sisalana

With its smooth leaf margins, *Agave sisalana* is quite decorative, especially if contrasted against white gravel.

Plants grow as medium-sized to large rosettes that produce many suckers from the base. The deep green leaves generally lack marginal spines.

After several years a massive, many-branched flowering pole is produced. The flowers are green and carried vertically on the side branches of the inflorescence. There is no seed, but thousands of plantlets are formed on the inflorescence.

As is often the case with agricultural crops, the Mexican *Agave sisalana* (sisal) has variable forms. The most popular horticultural forms have variegated leaves with white, longitudinal sections.

In parts of the world, *Agave sisalana* is grown in plantations, as the extracted, dried leaf fibers are used to produce ropes and mats.

Agave victoria-reginae

The rosettes of *Agave victoria-reginae* consist of short stubby leaves that are densely packed in a tight rosette.

These are small to medium-sized plants (at least for *Agave*), with tightly packed, very neat rosettes. These are typically ball-shaped, which gives them a pleasing appearance as their shape emulates that of some of the larger globular or barrel-shaped cacti.

The leaves are generally short and stubby with very sharp terminal spikes. The densely arranged leaves are striking, in that they are adorned with distinct white lines, or bud imprints, on both surfaces.

At maturity the plant produces a single unbranched, sturdy, robust inflorescence that hardly seems compatible with the comparatively small rosettes.

This species, which was named for Britain's Queen Victoria, is indigenous to Mexico. It is a most desirable plant to have in a collection.

Some of the forms of *Agave victoria-reginae* sucker freely, while others will remain as single rosettes.

In some forms of the species, the white lines on the leaves are rather faint. Understandably, the most popular forms among collectors are those that have their leaves adorned with robust white lines.

These plants are striking in any setting, with or without cacti. Care should be taken that plants are not overwatered; they succumb easily to fungal rot if the soil in which they grow is kept wet for prolonged periods.

Hesperaloe parviflora

In a healthy clump of *Hesperaloe parviflora* plants, the leaves form a tangled mass. The leaves have short, curled, white threadlike filaments on their margins. These plants do well in the open ground or in containers.

Plants grow as small to medium-sized clumps of slender-leaved rosettes. The leaves vary from dark to bluish green, with indistinct longitudinal lines on both surfaces. The leaf margins carry beautifully curled threadlike filaments.

A tall, branched inflorescence is produced in early to midsummer. Small clusters of open, *Aloe*-like flowers, varying from dull pink to deep, bright red, are carried on the inflorescence. After successful fertilization of the flowers, fat, bright green capsules filled with large, black seeds are produced.

Hesperaloe parviflora is native to northern Mexico and southwestern USA. The species shows considerable variation in its leaf and inflorescence characteristics. The latter can be tall and drooping, unable to support its own weight, or short and erect.

Propagation is through the division of clumps, or easily germinated seed.

Manfreda maculosa (sometimes treated as *Agave maculosa*)

Manfreda maculosa will rapidly spread in a bed to form rosulate clumps of highly colored leaves. Inset photo. The reflexed portions of the flower parts of *Manfreda maculosa* are golden brown.

Plants grow as a low, mat-like ground cover. They consist of small rosettes of fairly long, soft, floppy leaves that are deeply channeled. The leaves are uniformly dull green or have large, purplish brown blotches, particularly on the upper surfaces, and the leaf margins are finely sawtoothed.

The inflorescence is very long and carries large, open-mouthed flowers in a sparse arrangement. The flower buds are a muted green, while the open, reflexed floral parts are a golden brownish color.

This species originates from Mexico and the southern USA. Plants are deciduous, which means they die back to ground level during the winter months. In spring the leaves reemerge with fresh vigor.

The easiest way to propagate this species is by dividing existing clumps.

The leaves are quite brittle and can be easily damaged by pedestrian traffic.

Ruschia intricata

AIZOACEAE

The members of this, the largest of the world's succulent plant families, are fascinating in all respects. The family includes about 1,800 species; about as many cacti are recognized globally. While the cacti are mostly restricted to the western hemisphere, most aizooids that appeal to collectors are restricted to South Africa's western, winter rainfall area. They are typically leaf succulents, but some also have thick, swollen stems and/or roots. Furthermore, they show exceptional variation in terms of growth forms, ranging from tiny, water-filled plant bodies to small, much-branched trees.

The azooids, which are here interchangeably also referred to as mesembs, are still sometimes treated as belonging to the family Mesembryanthemaceae. Here a broader family concept is followed that includes the Mesembryanthemaceae, and a few other families, in the more inclusive Aizoaceae.

The flowers of the mesembs superficially resemble the head-shaped inflorescences of daisy plants. The fruits are interesting in that they open and close in response to moisture. When they get wet, during a downpour for example, seeds are dislodged from the fruit capsules, which close again once the rain stops, only to reopen during the next rain shower.

Three groups of mesembs are particularly popular among succulent-plant collectors: the representatives with pebble-shaped bodies (including *Lithops* spp.), ground cover that will quickly cover a denuded area, and the shrubs with brightly colored flowers, such as *Lampranthus* and *Ruschia* species.

In their natural habitats, the shrubby plants are often insignificant-looking, rather scraggly plants, but in cultivation they form nicely rounded canopies that are covered in flowers that can be virtually any color except blue and black!

In contrast, the plant bodies of the pebble plants, which are often two-leaved, are sunk into the ground in their habitats but, in cultivation, will rapidly take on a rather unnatural appearance as they respond to an abundance of water and comparatively low light intensities.

In warm climates, the shrubs should be planted out in the open where they are protected against too much water and very low temperatures. The stone plants often do much better in pots, where the amount of water they receive can be carefully controlled. In general, the mesembs are not very hardy in cold climates, as most species have soft leaves that are easily damaged by frost. Plants must be protected against frost and, especially those that originate in summer rainfall areas, from winter rain coupled with subzero temperatures.

Aptenia ×vascosilvae 'Red Apple'

The leaves of Aptenia ×vascosilvae 'Red Apple' are bright green and the flowers bright red.

Plants grow as soft-leaved creepers that will quickly cover a denuded area if small cuttings are planted a short distance apart. The green, angled stems are soft and somewhat brittle. Leaves are shield- to slightly heart-shaped and a pleasant, bright green color.

Flowers are bright strawberry red. Plants grow very easily in any mild climate and any soil type. It is also well adapted to be planted in soil pockets in retaining walls from where plants will trail down. It can be become invasive and material should not be discarded irresponsibly.

The main flowering time is February to August in the northern hemisphere. However, Aptenia ×vascosilvae has been observed to sporadically flower, often profusely, throughout the year.

Aptenia ×vascosilvae 'Red Apple' was selected from a hybrid between A. cordifolia and A. haeckeliana, two southern African species.

Carpobrotus edulis subsp. edulis

A dense stand of Carpobrotus edulis subsp. edulis.

Plants are heavy soil-huggers of which the stems remain prostrate, but will scramble into plants with which it is grown. The leaves are angled and rather short and fingerlike. Flowers are quite large and yellow, fading to somewhat pinkish as they wither. Fruit is fleshy and edible, but do not split open when they are dry.

Plants become naturalized very easily from discarded stems or from the seed that is easily dispersed by birds, for example.

Cheiridopsis purpurea

The stubby leaves of Cheiridopsis purpurea are a light bluish white color that strongly contrasts with the purple flowers.

Plants grow as small, branched tufts. The V-shaped, paired leaves are borne erectly at an angle and smooth-rounded along the back. Leaves are generally a beautiful light bluish to bluish white color. In some forms the leaves are distinctly and densely dotted with tiny darker spots.

In the dry season the leaves can become wrinkled, but will soon flesh out once irrigation is resumed in the growing season. Interestingly, in this species the petals usually do not fully unfold.

Delosperma purpureum

The flowers of *Delosperma purpureum* are bright, shiny purple.

Plants grow as small shrubs that can reach a height of about 12"–15" (30–40cm). However, the stems are weak and plants often sprawl along the ground. Leaves are short and cylindrical, and adorned with crystal-like cells—called bladder cells—on their surface.

Flowers are bright purple and often carried in profusion in the warm summer months. Given the soft texture of the leaves and stems, the plants can be easily trimmed and kept tidy. If cuttings are planted densely, this species makes a very useful ground cover.

Drosanthemum marinum

Like many other mesembs, the common name applied to most representatives of the family Aizoaceae, *Drosanthemum marinum* is a useful ground cover. The flowers of this form are nearly white, infused with pinkish purple.

Another very useful ground cover, *Drosanthemum marinum* is a low-growing creeper that that can serve as a lawn replacement in especially winter-wet/summer-dry climates. The leaves are short, baby finger-like and, with mild irrigation, a pleasant light green color. Flowers are whitish, but with a pinkish purple infusion. The base of the fruit is strongly adorned with decorative, crystal-like bladder cells.

Ebracteola wilmaniae

Ebracteola wilmaniae has green, fingerlike leaves dotted with dark spots. The flowers are pinkish purple with white sections.

Plants grow as very low clumps that have numerous fingerlike leaves exposed above ground.

The leaves are soft, and a pleasant sea green color, tinged with purplish pink, with numerous tiny, darker spots dotted all over them. The flowers are a light pink color, with white centers.

The species is indigenous to South Africa's interior savanna and grassland areas. In its natural habitat it is often found in the rather thin clay soils in rock depressions.

Ebracteola wilmaniae is propagated through division of the clumps. Seeds also germinate without difficulty. It prefers summer rain, and can tolerate a surprising amount of it if planted in open beds with good drainage.

Frithia humilis

The short, cylindrical leaves of *Frithia humilis* are flat on the apex, which, along with the patterning, has given rise to the common name "fairy elephant's feet."

In its natural habitat in central South Africa quite often only the flattened leaf tips of *Frithia humilis* are visible at ground level during the dry season. Unlike the vast majority of mesembs, this is a summer rainfall species. The leaves, when extended beyond ground level in the rainy season, are cylindrical and the surfaces are flat, windowed, and patterned.

Flowers are white with yellow centers. It has been shown that the leaves, rather than the roots, of the species are contractile, enabling the plants to contract underground. This miniature plant responds well to cultivation, especially when kept in a small container filled with a well-drained soil mixture.

Gibbaeum dispar

The flowers of *Gibbaeum dispar* are bright pink and quite large.

This is one of the many interesting miniature mesembs, a group that is also referred to as "living stones." Many have become very popular to keep in small containers on windowsills in harsh climates, and are highly prized as collector's items kept under glass.

The individual plant bodies of *Gibbaeum dispar* consist of only a few leaves that are arranged in opposite pairs. When young and solitary, plants are only about 1" (2.5cm) tall. With age, plants will form rounded, mound-like, leafy clumps of about 4" (10cm) in diameter. The leaves are a pleasant bluish green color and subtly angled.

The flowers are bright pink and quite large for the fairly small plant bodies. The species is indigenous to the Klein Karoo, a dry region in southern South Africa.

Lampranthus glaucus

Lampranthus glaucus produces an array of butter yellow flowers in the spring months.

Plants grow as small, manageable shrublets. The stems are thin and soft, especially when young. The slightly angled, cylindrical leaves are short with blunt tips and carried some distance apart on the purplish green stems.

The flowers are quite large and bright yellow. These are borne in profusion in spring.

The species is indigenous to coastal and adjacent inland parts of South Africa's Western Cape.

Plants remain as small shrublets but, if planted closely together, will form a continuous mat, producing an amazing display of golden yellow flowers.

Lithops lesliei subsp. *lesliei*

When fully expanded, the bright yellow flowers of *Lithops lesliei* subsp. *lesliei* completely obscure the plant body.

These small, button-shaped stone plants resemble the pebbles among which they grow. The plant bodies consist of two leaves that are fused basally, usually below ground level, with only the flattened tips exposed.

The visible leaf tips have interesting patterns and light-colored windows, giving rise to the common name, "window plants," which is sometimes applied to many different mesembs.

The bright yellow flowers are quite large. The plants become visible only once the flowers close at night, or during inclement weather.

Lithops lesliei has a preference for summer rainfall. It is widely distributed in the grasslands and adjacent areas of the South African interior.

Unlike many Aizoaceae, it does not mind clay soil. However, plants should not be left in wet, poorly drained soil for long periods.

A fascination with the strange shape, size, and outline of *Lithops* species is often the reason why people start succulent plant collections.

Pleiospilos compactus

Pleiospilos compactus, commonly known as "split rocks," bear large, yellow flowers.

Species of *Pleiospilos* are generally known as "liver plants" or "split rocks," a reference to their fat, rock-like leaves that are decorated with numerous small dots. The dwarf, stemless plant bodies consist of leaf pairs that are arranged oppositely. Each leaf is almost spherical, flattened above, and round-angled below. The leaves are divided by a deep split or fissure but they are connected at the base. In winter, a leaf pair will open with a new pair emerging from the center.

As the summer months approach, the leaves may take on a more reddish color. When fully expanded, the large, yellow flowers will almost completely hide the leaves. Plants should be sparingly watered in the summer months and kept fairly dry during winter. Like all species of mesemb that mimic the rocks among which they grow naturally, *P. compactus* is indigenous to the arid regions of southern Africa.

Most species of *Pleiospilos* do best in cultivation if kept in a container that provides sufficient space for the tap roots that will develop in time.

Rhombophyllum dolabriforme

The back of the leaves of *Rhombophyllum dolabriforme* are adorned with a prominent tooth-like protrusion.

Plants grow singly and will in time form small, densely branched tufts. The generally dull light green leaves are sickle-shaped and have prominent tooth-like extensions on their backs. In some forms of the species the leaf surface is prominently crystalline—these are usually the most striking forms of the species to cultivate.

Flowers are bright yellow and carried on rather long stalks for such small plants. Plants grow very well in containers.

Ruschia intricata

Ruschia intricata produces a myriad bright purple flowers in the summer months. The stems carry sharp spines.

Plants grow as medium-sized, rounded shrubs that consist of thin, stiff, somewhat woody stems and branches.

The leaves are very much reduced and cylindrical and the flowers are a striking, bright purple color.

Rushia intricata, previously and widely known as *Eberlanzia spinosa*, is indigenous to the central karroid and grassland regions of South Africa.

Thorns are not the main defense mechanism used by most mesemb species. However, *Ruschia intricata* has exceptionally sharp, stiff thorns that are sure to cause discomfort to an unobservant passerby.

This species is exceptionally cold hardy, and subzero temperatures do it no harm whatsoever.

Pachypodium lamerei

APOCYNACEAE

The inclusion of the well-known carrion flower family, the Asclepiadaceae, in the more diverse, and now much larger, family Apocynaceae is nowadays widely accepted. The genus *Stapelia*, the name of which has become accepted as a common name for many representatives of the family, as stapeliads, is perhaps the best known of the carrion flower genera. The stapeliads and their numerous generic relatives are essentially stem succulents with smooth or hairy surfaces, but some, at least, also have succulent leaves (for example, representatives of *Ceropegia*) and/or caudices (for example, representatives of *Brachystelma*).

Few succulent plants can boast such intriguing flowers as characterize the stapeliads, whose internal and external surfaces often sport small, tendril-like appendages that will break into motion at the slightest breeze, emulating fungal threads. The flowers often appear oversized for the fairly small size of the plants and many are in muted shades of russet and purple. In addition to the intricacies of the flowers' structure, the succulent representatives of the family have a further claim to fame: their flowers smell like decaying meat. They are adapted for insect pollination, which is often performed by bluebottles (blowflies) and house flies.

Most representatives of the family Apocynaceae occur naturally in temperate regions that experience either summer or winter rainfall in fairly limited amounts. However, none of these regions are subjected to the severely cold, wet conditions prevalent in colder climates. They should therefore be kept in heated (ideally) or unheated (risky) greenhouses.

Apart from the stapeliads, the Apocynaceae, quite a large plant family as presently circumscribed, includes species that used to be classified on their own in this family, such as *Adenium*. As a further example, the frangipanis, with their sweet-smelling flowers, are included in this subdivision of the Apocynaceae.

Hoodia pilifera subsp. annulata

The erect stems of *Hoodia pilifera* subsp. *annulata* closely resemble those of cactus plants. During the flowering season, they are covered with chocolate brown flowers.

Plants grow as large clumps of cactus-like stems. The stems are a grayish white color, leafless and covered with spinelike protuberances.

The flowers are a deep chocolate brown color and quite large.

It is best to grow the species from seed as stem cuttings do not root that easily.

The species is very particular as far as watering is concerned and care should be taken not to overwater plants in cultivation.

This species is indigenous to South Africa's arid interior, particularly the karroid regions.

Hoya carnosa

The flowers of *Hoya carnosa* are carried in ball-shaped inflorescences.

Commonly known as the wax plant or wax flower, *Hoya carnosa* has become very popular over the past few years for growing indoors, even in fairly low-light conditions. The leaves are thickened and waxy and the star-shaped flowers, which are carried in clusters the size and shape of a tennis ball, similarly have a distinctive, waxy appearance. The leaves are uniformly dark green or are variously mottled with golden yellow or silvery flecks of different shapes and sizes.

Once planted, plants should be left to grow in that container and ideally not be repotted for a long while, as disturbance to the roots can significantly slow down the plants' growth.

Plants benefit from occasional feeding with a liquid organic fertilizer. It is a very useful plant to grow in a hanging basket.

Huernia thuretii

The star-shaped flowers of *Huernia thuretii* are quite large for the small, tufted plants.

These low-growing plants are essentially creeping succulents that consist of short, fat stems. The stems are distinctly angled, and carry small, harmless protuberances along the rib margins. The fairly large, star-shaped flowers are yellow with numerous red spots and are foul-scented. Plants flower in summer.

The species is widespread in the eastern parts of South Africa. It responds well to cultivation and can easily be divided to multiply the material being grown.

Orbea lutea subsp. *lutea*

The bright yellow, foul-smelling flowers of *Orbea lutea* subsp. *lutea* are borne in small clusters near the tips of the stems.

Plants grow as small clumps of creeping stems that can cover quite large areas. The angled stems carry numerous harmless, spinelike protuberances on their margins. The flowers, produced in small clusters, are mostly uniformly yellow, and foul-smelling.

The species has a wide geographical distribution, and occurs naturally in South Africa's interior savanna region.

Orbea lutea subsp. *lutea* is easy to cultivate from stem cuttings. The plants often creep along the ground toward suitable microenvironments where they can flourish, such as a shady corner under surrounding plants.

This species produces some of the strongest smelling flowers of all the asclepiads.

Pachypodium geayi

The usually single-stemmed Malagasy *Pachypodium geayi* often branches higher up after it has flowered. The leaves are silvery. Plants are readily available in nurseries and grow very well in virtually any mild climate.

Plants have a columnar to slightly bottle-shaped growth form, with the stems often remaining unbranched for many years before the growing tip will divide once it has flowered. The stems are beautifully adorned with symmetrically arranged clusters of sharp spines. The leaves of this Malagasy species can reach a length of up to about 16" (40cm) long and are a grayish green color with the leaf margins being rolled down. The flowers are white.

Plants grow well in mild-climate parts of the world, especially where winter freezes do not occur. They can even be planted in rather small containers and will grow well, if somewhat stunted, for many years.

Pachypodium lamerei

Pachypodium lamerei has white flowers that fade to light brown when older.

The densely spiny stems gradually taper upward from a bottle-like, rounded base, and after plants have flowered, the stems will branch, with clusters of bright green, slightly leathery leaves carried toward the apices. Flowers are quite large, white, and fade to light brown before they are shed.

This species has become very popular as a container plant to place on verandas away from pedestrian traffic. Plants grow very easily—more so than the look-alike *P. geayi*—and must rate as the most widely grown of all the pachypodiums.

Where temperatures dip below freezing in winter, plants should be provided with protection.

Stapelia gigantea

In the summer months, *Stapelia gigantea* produces numerous very large flowers that are the color of rotting meat.

Plants grow as clumps of short, erect, fingerlike stems, which are velvety and angled. Short, stubby protuberances occur along the edges of the angles.

The flowers are a deep brick red color and are produced throughout the hot summer months.

The species is indigenous to South Africa's savanna interior, where they grow under the protection of rocks and bushes. Seed germination is profuse, but stem cuttings, which root easily, are the preferred method of propagation.

This is arguably the most widely grown of all the carrion flowers. The flowers are very large; in fact they are the largest single flowers encountered among succulent plants globally.

Stapelia leendertziae

The flowers of *Stapelia leendertziae* are shaped like wine glasses and are a deep wine red color.

Plants form large sweeps that consist of numerous, closely packed stems that reach a height of about 6" (15cm). The stems are light to bluish green, rather narrow, and along their edges carry small, harmless protuberances. Flowers are finely and transversely ridged on the inside surfaces and are a deep wine red color. The strongly foul-scented flowers are additionally shaped like large wine goblets.

Clumps of the plant can be easily divided and the resulting cuttings planted on. The species does well in dappled shade and in full sun.

Kumara plicatilis

ASPHODELACEAE

All representatives of the subfamily Alooideae of the Asphodelaceae, (sometimes accorded family status as the Aloaceae), have succulent leaves variously arranged into rosettes. Indeed, aloes have a growth form not unlike that of agaves, but they are long-lived perennials that will flower regularly year after year, once they have reached reproductive maturity.

With the exception of representatives of the genera *Haworthia*, *Haworthiopsis*, *Tulista*, and *Astroloba*, their flowers are brightly colored, and many species bear a succession of red, orange, or yellow torches during a single flowering season. They tend to flower in winter when many of their companion plants are in a drab, resting phase.

Depending on the preferred classification, the *Aloe* subfamily consists of up to 11 genera. The aloes and their close relatives are nowadays arranged into the following genera: *Aloe* (true aloes), *Aloidendron* (tree aloes), *Kumara* (fan aloes), *Aloiampelos* (rambling aloes), *Aristaloe* (awn-leaf aloe), *Gonialoe* (*kanniedood* aloes), *Gasteria* (gasterias), *Astroloba* (astrolobas), *Haworthia* (haworthias), *Haworthiopsis* (angled haworthias), and *Tulista* (robust haworthias). However, the species most widely cultivated belong to three major genera: *Aloe*, *Haworthia*, and *Gasteria*. Most representatives of this family are easily damaged by subzero temperatures. They will certainly require protection against frosty conditions, especially if grown in areas that receive excessive rainfall.

Flowers of *Gasteria* species are about the size of most *Aloe* species, but they tend to be curved and shaped like small bananas. Perhaps, most characteristically, the flowers of the majority of the species have a basal, bulb-like swelling. Their leaves are often tongue-shaped, and the leaf margins armed with a horny edge.

In contrast, representatives of *Haworthia* and its generic relatives have small, mostly nondescript, muted white flowers, and small rosettes of *Aloe*-like leaves. The fascinating leaf shapes and textures of *Haworthia* species are major reasons for their popularity among succulent collectors.

The other subfamily of the Asphodelaceae, the Asphodeloideae, includes the red hot pokers (*Kniphofia* species), representatives of which prefer moist habitats. Only some genera of this group, such as *Bulbine*, have fat, water-filled leaves.

Aloe arborescens

Aloe arborescens, a perennial favorite, produces a profusion of brightly colored inflorescences during the winter, although summer-flowering forms are known. This is cultivar 'Estelle Potgieter.'

These many-branched, robust shrubs consist of numerous rosettes carried on stems clothed in the remains of dried leaves. The leaves are generally sickle-shaped, with short, stout but fairly harmless teeth.

Each rosette bears one or more inflorescences, the shape of fiery cones, and consisting of pencil-shaped flowers that vary from red through orange to yellow.

The stems and rosettes tend to be tightly packed, resulting in a beautiful, rounded plant with a neat appearance, that can be planted almost anywhere in a garden, or in a container.

The wide distribution range, from coastal dunes to high altitudes, indicates that selected forms will flourish in many different climates.

Aloe ×commutata

Aloe ×commutata flowers prolifically during spring.

Plants are stemless or may in time produce very short stems on top of which the strong rosettes are perched. Leaves are short and triangular-deltoid, and along the margins are armed with short, brown, pungent, generally recurved or straight teeth. Leaf color is generally dull dark green with numerous white, H-shaped spots conspicuously scattered on the upper surface; the lower surface tends to be milky green. The apical portions of the leaves tend to die back.

Flower color is consistently a bright orange-red. *Aloe ×commutata* is widely naturalized in the Mediterranean region of Europe.

Aloe comptonii

Aloe comptonii is an ideal plant to grow against a near-vertical cliff face or a dry rock wall in a flowerbed.

Plants grow as single or, rarely, double-branched erect or creeping individuals. The leaves are incurved and a dull bluish green color. The remains of the old, dry leaves tend to cover most of the stems. The teeth on the leaf margins are short, stout, and distinctly white in color.

The species has a fairly long flowering season in late winter and early spring. The flowers are quite long and carried in distinctly head-shaped inflorescences.

Aloe comptonii inhabits the mountains and rocky outcrops in South Africa's Little Karoo, an arid region in the central-south of the country.

With its short, creeping stems, the species is well adapted to growing against rock faces. In addition, it has few rivals if it is spring color that is desired in a garden.

Horticulturally, the species does equally well in warmer regions that receive winter and summer rain.

Aloe ferox

Aloe ferox grows in dry climates and doesn't need a lot of water. Inset photo. The inflorescences are multibranched and arranged in a candelabra-like fashion.

Plants grow as robust, single-stemmed specimens that carry a single, large rosette. The stems are typically clothed in skirts of dry, boat-shaped leaves with strong teeth on the margins. Some forms, especially those that occur in the Western Cape of South Africa, also have teeth on both leaf surfaces.

The inflorescences are multibranched. The flowers, which range in color from pure white through orange and yellow to bright red, are tightly packed in the strikingly beautiful, torch-like inflorescences, which are borne in winter when few other plants are in flower.

Plants are exceptionally drought tolerant and also able to withstand low, dry temperatures. The skirt of dry leaves should not be removed from cultivated specimens, as it makes for much more natural-looking plants if the leaves are retained.

Extracts of the thick, juice-filled *Aloe ferox* leaves are used in health drinks, skin lotions, and shampoos.

Aloe lineata var. lineata

Aloe lineata var. *lineata*, which forms large multistemmed, bushy plants, is a perfect aloe to grow in coastal gardens.

Plants often grow as multistemmed clusters, with plantlets and secondary branches clustered along the stem.

The leaves are narrow and sword-shaped, with distinct reddish longitudinal lines. Both upper and lower surfaces are smooth and dull green, and the margins are armed with sharp teeth.

The inflorescences appear blunt-tipped as a result of the long floral leaves that protect the buds. The fairly long flowers vary in color from deep orange to dull pinkish orange.

The species thrives in protected pockets of subtropical thicket in South Africa's Eastern Cape, from sea level to somewhat inland. In cultivation it does very well in both summer and winter rainfall areas.

Aloe maculata

Aloe maculata's wide distribution range extends from South Africa's Western Cape to Eswatini (Swaziland) and beyond.

Plants grow as small to medium-sized rosettes; either singly or arranged in multiheaded clusters. The leaves are mostly short and deltoid, and the margins have short, sharp teeth. Both surfaces are mottled with light green to whitish flecks in the shape of an "H."

The flowers have very distinct ball-shaped swellings at the base, and are carried in flat-topped inflorescences.

This species has one of the widest natural distribution ranges of all *Aloe* species, transcending the boundaries of southern Africa's summer and winter rainfall regions, and confirming its usefulness as a horticultural subject in virtually any setting.

Flowering is variable, with plants flowering throughout the seasons.

Aloe marlothii

Aloe marlothii, a typical savanna species, grows as a single, unbranched plant, but can be kept small in a pot.

Plants grow as large, single-stemmed specimens with a robust rosette at the top of a stem clothed in the remains of dead leaves. The large, boat-shaped leaves have teeth along their margins and, most commonly, on both surfaces.

The multibranched inflorescences are carried horizontally. The tubular flowers, borne vertically, vary in color, being uniformly bright red, orange, or bi-colored (orange-yellow; red-white).

This is a typical savanna species of the southern Africa interior. In some parts of its natural distribution range it is exceedingly common and, when in flower, lights up the hillsides with its striking colors. It is a summer rainfall species that can last an entire winter with very little rain.

Aloe ×nobilis

In midsummer *Aloe ×nobilis* produces a multitude of inflorescences.

Plants remain low-growing and will in time form dense mats of closely packed rosettes. The leaves are fairly short and usually quite stubby, a dark green color, and carry short, white, harmless prickles along the margins. The inflorescences are rather diffusely flowered with bright orangey red, pencil-shaped flowers. Flowers are produced in midsummer, a time when few other aloes are in flower.

The species is exceedingly easy in cultivation in winter rainfall regions, such as in Mediterranean climates. It has become naturalized in some countries in southern Europe.

Aloe peglerae

Aloe peglerae's small, ball-shaped rosettes support short, stout strikingly beautiful inflorescences in the spring.

Plants grow as solitary, small to medium-sized, ball-shaped rosettes. The bluish green leaves are sickle-shaped and incurved. The leaf margins are densely toothed, while the surfaces may also carry scattered teeth.

The inflorescences are carried on very short stalks that hardly protrude above the rosettes, giving the inflorescences the appearance of rockets being launched from blue globes.

The species originates from a small part of South Africa's savanna grasslands, above the climatically severe inland escarpment.

As a result of the plants' beauty, *Aloe peglerae* has been targeted by illegal collectors for some time. This has resulted in an alarming decline in the number of plants remaining in their natural habitat.

Aloe 'Peri Peri'

In this garden bed the light bluish green leaves and red flowers of *Aloe* 'Peri Peri' contrast with the white rocks used as an inorganic mulch.

Plants of this cultivar grow as small to medium-sized rosettes that sprout numerous plants from the base. The leaves are carried erectly, with the upper third curved outward. The leaves are a bluish green color and carry stiff but harmless white prickles along the margins. Often multibranched inflorescences carry bright red, cigar-shaped flowers in elongated candles.

Plants flower profusely during the early winter months. *Aloe* 'Peri Peri' has become a very popular garden aloe.

Aloe pratensis

Aloe pratensis occurs naturally in some of the coldest parts of southern Africa, usually favoring rocky outcrops amid the grasslands.

Plants grow as small, stemless, open rosettes. The leaves are a striking bluish green color, and the leaf margins and leaf surfaces are adorned with stout teeth.

The compact growth form and robust inflorescence of this aloe have contributed to its popularity among collectors, resulting in plants being removed illegally from their natural habitats. Sadly, the species does not transplant well and wild collected material almost invariably dies an agonizingly slow death in cultivation.

The species grows naturally in the Eastern Cape grassland areas. Its distribution range includes some of the coldest parts of southern Africa, including the foothills and higher ground of the Drakensberg mountains in the Eastern Cape and Lesotho.

ABOUT ALOES

The vast majority of species of *Aloe* occur in the summer rainfall regions of Africa. These species mainly flower during the dry winter months. This enables the plants to disperse their almost invariably small, black, wingless seeds during the ensuing months, just in time for the summer rains to facilitate seed germination and the establishment of the small seedlings with their initially very weak root systems. The opposite is of course true for some of the winter rainfall aloes, such as the spring-to-summer-flowering South African Tree-fan Aloe, *Kumara plicatilis*, which is restricted to the unique fynbos vegetation.

The horticultural benefit of the winter flowering of most *Aloe* species is that they provide magnificent splashes of color in domestic gardens during the drab winter months when little else is in flower, although they do need protection from frost.

MORE ABOUT ALOES . . .

Aloes come in all shapes and sizes. Their growth forms range from miniature rosette plants to massive trees of over 65 ft. (20m) tall, and everything in between. The succulent creepers, *Aloiampelos tenuior* and *Aloiampelos ciliaris*, are scramblers that will form large mounds of tangled, leafy stems dotted with bright yellow or red flowers in sparse to dense clusters. These two species, and some others, such as *Aloiampelos striatula*, are the lazy succulent gardener's stalwarts, as they require little care, but just keep on flowering year after year without fail.

Aloe striata

The common name of *Aloe striata*, "coral aloe," is quite apt as the leaves are a pleasant sea green color and the leaf margins have a pink rim.

Plants are fairly low-growing, but in time will develop into short, shrubby specimens of which the stems remain clothed in the dried remains of dead leaves. The beautifully bluish- to sea green (turquoise) colored leaves are faintly striped, and have distinct light pinkish margins.

The many-branched inflorescences are usually flat-topped, and carry small, bright orange flowers in dense clusters in spring.

This is a species of South Africa's Eastern Cape and arid karroo regions. The flowers give color to the landscape at a time when few aloes are in flower, making it a desirable acquisition for any garden.

These plants do not have a seasonal preference for rainfall, and can tolerate downpours at any time of the year. It is a good plant for coastal gardens.

Aloe vera

In this protected corner on a veranda in Golegã, central Portugal, a potted specimen of *Aloe vera* contrasts with the shadows cast on the privacy walls by the peripheral pillars. Inset photo. An inflorescence of yellow-flowered *Aloe vera*.

Plants of *Aloe vera* grow very well in open beds or in pots and, given its use as a medicinal plant, the species is easily the most widely cultivated aloe globally. It has become naturalized in various parts of the world, is grown in vast plantations for the harvesting of its leaf juices, and is also popular as a windowsill plant in a small pot, where it will flourish for many years.

Clumps can be easily divided to multiply plants. The leaves are soft, light green, and sometimes have diffusely scattered small, white spots on both surfaces. Inflorescences are single or could be branched. The cigar-shaped flowers are yellow, although forms with orangey flowers are known.

Aloiampelos ciliaris var. ciliaris

A cluster of *Aloiampelos ciliaris* var. *ciliaris* stems. Inset photo. The inflorescences of *A. ciliaris* var. *ciliaris* rarely branch, as here.

Plants grow as dense clusters of thin stems that will clamber into and onto plants with which it grows, or can be trained onto a trellis. The stems can easily reach a length of 18 ft. (6m), but can also be cut back to allow the plants to sprout from the base. The leaves are thinly succulent and rather flimsy. The leaf bases are adorned with conspicuous hair-like cilia—hence the scientific name of the species—where they clasp the stems.

Usually unbranched inflorescences are generally borne in the colder months, but plants can flower at other times of the year. Flowers are quite long and carried in short, dense, or slightly elongated inflorescences and are bright red.

Aristaloe aristata

Plants of *Aristaloe aristata* will soon divide to give rise to large clusters of ball-shaped rosettes. Flowers are dull pinkish orange.

Plants are the size—and often the shape—of tennis balls, and the leaves curl inwards when under drought stress. Several different forms of the species are known, with most responding very well to cultivation.

The leaves are small and densely adorned with white prickles on both surfaces and along the margins. Flowers are very large for the small size of the plants, dull pinkish orange to yellowish orange, and usually curved like bananas toward the flowering stalk.

A clump of *Aristaloe aristata* happily growing and flowering in a pot on a windowsill of a shuttered window in Rio Maior in central Portugal. An edible leaf succulent, *Portulaca oleracea* (coin-shaped leaves on the left), is also growing in the pot.

Bulbine latifolia

Bulbine latifolia has an aloe-like rosette. Inset photo. The flowers are tightly packed in a narrowly cone-shaped inflorescence.

Unlike the stiff, turgid, marginally toothed leaves of the vast majority of the aloes, those of *Bulbine latifolia* are soft and firm but pliable and lack any armature along the margins. The leaves are light green to light yellowish green and are carried in a rosette. Plants can in time develop a short stem that remains clothed in the remains of drying leaves.

Yellow flowers are arranged in a narrowly cone-shaped inflorescence; hairs on the stamens give the flowers a fluffy appearance. Seed germinates easily and is the preferred method to ensure a next crop of the species.

Gasteria acinacifolia

A large clump of *Gasteria acinacifolia* growing near the beach. Inset photo. *Gasteria acinacifolia* flowers are quite large and have only slight basal swellings.

Plants grow as very large, mostly single, rosettes. The leaves are very broad, with an oblique keel that stretches toward their tips, to give the leaves a typically triangular outline in cross-section.

The large flowers hang from horizontal inflorescence branches. They are bright orange, tinged with yellow.

The species is indigenous to South Africa's Eastern Cape coast. In its natural habitat it is most commonly encountered in low-growing dune scrub that is as high as the tops of the large rosettes. The climate where it occurs naturally is quite mild, and the species is unable to tolerate very low temperatures.

Propagation is by means of seed that germinates easily, or by removing and rooting some of the basal suckers. New plants will also develop when a single leaf is placed in a suitable rooting medium such as gritty sand.

In nature, the plants are often subjected to moisture-laden sea wind and so they benefit from regular spraying when they are cultivated.

Gasteria bicolor var. bicolor

The mottled leaves of Gasteria bicolor var. bicolor are the perfect camouflage to foil browsers.

Plants usually grow as small to medium-sized, solitary rosettes that only rarely, very slowly, sucker from the base to form multiheaded specimens. The rosettes are almost invariably twisted into a spiral.

The leaves are usually quite long, dark green, and densely mottled with light green to whitish spots.

The small pinkish flowers are basally swollen and carried in large open inflorescences.

This native of South Africa's southeast coast has beautifully colored leaves that give it an immense ability to blend in with its surroundings.

This is a useful survival strategy, as gasterias lack the bitter substance present in the leaves of some aloes that deter browsers.

It prefers dappled shade and will grow perfectly well under trees with open canopies.

The species grows quite quickly and flowers regularly once it has reached flowering maturity.

It can be propagated by removing and rooting the basal suckers, but it is also easy to propagate from seed.

Gasteria disticha var. disticha

A specimen of Gasteria disticha var. disticha growing in the shade of surrounding plants.

This is one of the medium-sized gasterias that will sprout new plants from the base to form tightly packed clusters. It has its leaves arranged in a single row; the leaves are dark green, variously white-spotted, and rough to the touch. Leaf margins are adorned with small, flat, white tubercles that become confluent to give them a knife edge-like appearance.

Plants produce fairly large, dangling, pinkish green flowers in spring and summer, a time when their kin, true aloes, are not in flower. The species generally grows under xerophytic shrubs, so benefitting from the dappled shade.

Gasteria 'Little Warty'

The leaves of Gasteria 'Little Warty' have prominent milky green sections. Inset photo. The flowers are basally pinkish white and greenish white higher up.

Several cultivars have been described in *Gasteria*, generally based on hybrids between two or more species. The cultivars identifiable as belonging to the 'Little Warty' cluster have warty leaves, which likely indicate that *Gasteria carinata*, which has coarse leaf surfaces, is represented in its genetic makeup. The leaves furthermore have distinct light, milky green sections that make the plants very attractive.

The slightly curved flowers are basally pinkish white and greenish white toward the tips.

Gasteria 'Little Warty' is perfectly adapted for growing in containers and cluster at the base. These sprouts can be removed with a sharp knife and planted on.

Gonialoe variegata

Gonialoe variegata, the "partridge-breasted aloe," has been common in European greenhouses for several centuries.

Plants are well known as small, low-growing solitary specimens, but will readily form fairly large, multiheaded clumps. The leaves are reminiscent of species of *Gasteria*, being a fairly dark, blackish green, with irregular white spots. They are triangular in cross-section and compacted into three rows. The leaf margins carry a continuous white strip (as one finds in many gasterias).

The inflorescences carry the flowers in lax racemes. The dull pink to red flowers are somewhat curved.

Gonialoe variegata originates from South Africa's arid Karoo, where it grows under bushes that shield it from the intense sunlight. The plants can withstand extreme temperatures, but can easily be killed with too much water.

This is a widely cultivated species, with many European collections boasting a "partridge-breasted aloe."

Haworthia cymbiformis var. cymbiformis

A young specimen of *Haworthia cymbiformis* var. *cymbiformis* flowers for the first time.

The small, aloe-like rosettes remain low-growing, but plants will in time form mound-shaped clusters consisting of numerous rosettes. Leaves are soft and a light green color and especially toward the apices are adorned with longitudinally arranged, variously translucent, windows. Flowers are distinctly two-lipped and bright white.

Plants grow very well in small containers and can be easily propagated by dividing the clumps. In the areas where the variety grows naturally in South Africa's Eastern Cape, rainfall is predominantly in spring and autumn. As with many species from this area, plants can flower sporadically at any time of the year.

Haworthia maughanii

In cultivation, the leaves of *Haworthia maughanii* usually protrude above soil level, especially in the growing season.

The small cluster of leaves is arranged in a spiral with, in its natural habitat of the arid Klein Karoo in southern South Africa, only the flattened leaf tips being visible at soil level. The leaf tips are windowed with the windows often beautifully patterned. The round leaf tips furthermore make the species hard to detect in its natural habitat as they resemble the small rocks and pebbles among which they often grow. The two-lipped flowers are white.

Plants are easy in cultivation provided they are grown in a well-draining mixture and not overwatered.

Haworthiopsis attenuata

Haworthiopsis attenuata stands out in a single pot because of its deep green leaves with white "stripes."

Plants are strongly clustered and form large mats of low-growing rosettes that consist of tightly packed miniature dagger-shaped leaves. The leaves are deep green and crossbanded on both surfaces with prominent white ridge-like striations.

The inflorescences usually exceed the rosettes by several inches and often fail to support the flowers, which are a dull grayish white and distinctly two-lipped.

Plants do well in containers or as a ground cover in open beds. It is one of the most common *Haworthiopsis* species in the horticultural trade and a good one with which to gain confidence to start a succulent collection, as it is easy to grow and rapidly offsets, giving rise to large clumps.

Like many species from South Africa's Eastern Cape region, it has a year-round growing cycle.

Haworthiopsis fasciata

Haworthiopsis fasciata can be distinguished from *Haworthiopsis attenuata* by its smooth upper leaf surfaces.

Plants are often solitary but can also branch to form specimens with two or more heads. The light, dull green leaves are tightly packed along a short stem, to which they remain attached, even when dry. The upper leaf surfaces are completely smooth, while the lower surfaces are crossbanded with thin, white ridges. The flowers are an insignificant grayish white color.

This species originates from the Eastern Cape of South Africa where it grows with a multitude of other succulent species. It tends to favor a slightly acidic soil mixture.

The name *Haworthiopsis fasciata* has often been misapplied to the more common *Haworthiopsis attenuata*. However, the two species are easy to separate on leaf characters alone, as *Haworthiopsis fasciata* leaves have smooth upper surfaces and are more deltoid in shape.

Haworthiopsis glabrata

Haworthiopsis glabrata truly looks like a small species of aloe, with its rosettes and thickened leaves.

Plants grow as small, strongly clumping rosettes. The leaves are thickened and a light green color. Both the upper and lower surfaces of the leaves are covered with small whitish to uniformly green protuberances. The flowers are a dull whitish green color.

This species originates from the Eastern Cape of South Africa.

Along with *Haworthiopsis attenuata*, this is arguably the best species of the genus for the budding succulent enthusiast to start with, as it is remarkably non-fussy as far as soil type, watering regime, and temperature extremes are concerned.

Haworthiopsis viscosa

Leaves of the *Haworthiopsis viscosa* grow close together, almost seeming to connect along the stems.

Plants are immensely proliferous from the base and will form very large clumps of tightly packed stems.

The leaves are very short, slightly to distinctly recurved and a bright yellow color if exposed to full sun.

The flowers are grayish white and distinctly two-lipped.

This species, from the arid, south-central parts of South Africa's Klein Karoo, has a striking golden yellow leaf color if grown in hard conditions.

The elongated rosettes of *Haworthiopsis viscosa* can be easily removed and grown on to give rise to new plants. This is, in fact, the preferred method of propagation, even though the small, black seeds germinate easily.

Kumara plicatilis

A small specimen of *Kumara plicatilis* grown in a potbellied plant container.

The fan aloe, as this species is commonly known, grows into small to medium-sized, multibranched specimens that develop a corky bark on the stems and branches—an adaptation to the fire-prone natural habitats where it grows naturally in South Africa's Western Cape.

The light bluish green leaves are arranged in a single row and, in the flowering season, from between the leaves, a cone-shaped inflorescence is produced. The flowers are orange red and cigar-shaped. Plants are very easy in cultivation in winter rainfall regions, such as in California, and do well as pot plants or in open beds.

Tulista pumila

In its natural habitat, *Tulista pumila* receives winter rain. In summer, the soil is often dry for long periods, making for very desiccated-looking plants.

Plants usually grow as small, but large for the haworthioids, solitary rosettes. The leaves are usually strongly incurved, sometimes making the rosettes appear ball-shaped. They vary considerably in color, from light green to reddish brown; the latter color coming out in strong sunlight.

The inflorescence is much-branched and carries numerous, small, grayish white flowers.

Many forms and horticultural selections make this species a desirable acquisition for any collection. Their charm comes mainly from the variously shaped, dirty white to bright white tubercles carried on the leaves.

A number of well-entrenched names have been applied to this species, which is indigenous to the Worcester area of South Africa's Western Cape, including *Haworthia margaritifera* and *Haworthia pumila*. Now known as *Tulista pumila*, it is one of the smaller of the *Aloe* relatives; *pumila* means small.

×Senecurio kleiniiformis

ASTERACEAE

The Asteraceae, the largest family of flowering plants, has a near-universal geographical distribution range. To many aspiring collectors, the daisy family is not immediately associated with a succulent life form, but a surprisingly large number of species of this family are indeed stem and/or leaf succulents.

Members of the family occur in large numbers on most continents, where their head-shaped inflorescences often contribute to mass outdoor floral displays, one of the best-known examples being the mass spring flowering of daisies in western South Africa's Namaqualand, an arid inland region that has a distinct winter rainfall regime.

Many species of Asteraceae occur in temperate areas that are not subjected to severe climatic extremes. In colder climates, it is advisable to keep most of them in a greenhouse where the plants can benefit from some form of heating during winter.

The most desirable succulent species of Asteraceae used to be included in two genera, *Senecio* and *Kleinia*. These are now split across several daisy genera. The differences between these genera are not always obvious, as they are mostly based on cryptic differences in the morphology of the reproductive structures.

Many daisies are important in the horticultural trade, including South Africa's *Gerbera* species (Barberton daisies), and cultivars derived from them. Other daisy species, such as *Helianthus annuus* (the sunflower) and *Lactuca sativa* (lettuce) are important agricultural crops.

Caputia medley-woodii

The inflorescences of *Caputia medley-woodii* carry bright yellow, recurved ray florets.

The plants grow as robust shrubs that will either create a medium-sized, eye-catching feature on their own, or will scramble high into neighboring plants or shrubs. The leaves, which are fairly thick and whitish in color, are strikingly woolly and loosely arranged along the somewhat purplish stems.

The tiny flowers are arranged in head-shaped inflorescences, of which the ray florets have long, fused, recurved, butter yellow petals.

The species is indigenous to some of the densely wooded areas along South Africa's eastern seaboard. It is a handsome plant that grows easily from stem cuttings.

Surprisingly, it can withstand low temperatures, making it suitable for planting in colder areas.

Caputia tomentosa

The beauty of *Caputia tomentosa* is undoubtedly in the color of the leaves, which will perfectly complement a trendy, modern white garden.

Plants grow as small to medium-sized shrubs. The stems are slightly rough to the touch and gray in color. The upper parts of the stems and branches carry finger-shaped dull gray to pure white leaves that easily drop if the plant is not handled with care.

The inflorescences are fairly small and a dull whitish yellow.

It is worth giving this species a place in any dry succulent or cactus garden. It is a South African native that grows very easily from stem cuttings that can be placed directly in the intended spot in a garden. As it is very drought-tolerant, it will thrive with little or no aftercare.

Plants must be given strong sunlight to bring out the best in their white leaf color. Also, if they grow in the shade, the stems of the plants tend to topple over. *Caputia tomentosa* has been known under various names, of which *Senecio haworthii* was perhaps the most widely used.

Kleinia stapeliiformis

The stems of the succulent daisy, *Kleinia stapeliifomis*, closely resemble those of any number of carrion flower species, members of the Apocynaceae.

The stems of the plants are a deep brownish green, distinctly angled, and adorned with vertical rows of non-pungent protuberances.

Plants are leafless, but when they flower, there is no doubt that they belong to the daisy family. The bright red head-shaped inflorescences are borne on long stalks and attract attention from afar, even though ray florets are absent.

The species is indigenous to South Africa's savannas, where the prevalent climate is fairly mild. It makes a useful ground cover as, over time, it will proliferate by means of underground runners. Like all the *Kleinia* species, it requires a frost-free environment if it is to survive cold northern winters.

The specific epithet of the species name is very apt: when not in flower, the plants look uncannily like species of the carrion flower family.

Senecio barbertonicus

At first sight, *Senecio barbertonicus* looks like a pencil-bush euphorbia, but when in flower, the inflorescences clearly belong to the Asteraceae family.

Plants grow as typical, bushy shrubs that can reach the dimensions of small trees. The crowns are many-branched and quite dense. The leaves are a light green color and finger-shaped.

The head-shaped inflorescences are slender and borne erectly. They consist of tightly packed, bright yellow disk florets that lack conspicuous ray florets, but are nevertheless eye-catching.

Senecio barbertonicus, an inhabitant of the savanna or bushveld areas of southern Africa, is easy to cultivate in mild and subtropical regions, but cannot tolerate subzero temperatures.

Propagation is by means of stem cuttings that root rapidly in a friable, well-drained soil mixture.

Senecio crassissimus

The young stems of *Senecio crassissimus* are light green, but soon become purple-infused. The leaves are flexed vertically. Inset photo. The small, bright yellow flowers are carried in dense head-shaped clusters.

Plants grow as small to medium-sized shrubs that consist of numerous, erect to leaning, somewhat brittle stems. The young stems are light green, but soon become infused with a shade of purple. Interestingly, the leaves are flexed vertically rather than horizontally, which has given rise to one of its common names, "propeller plant." Along their edges, the leaves are often conspicuously purple colored. Leaf blades are thickly succulent and a silvery green color.

The bright yellow flowers are of two types: small disk florets, and ray florets with conspicuous petals. *Senecio crassissimus* is from Madagascar.

Senecio tamoides

The bright yellow inflorescences of *Senecio tamoides* are carried in dense, ball-shaped clusters.

Plants grow as large, multistemmed creepers that will rapidly cover a supporting structure, such as a trellis. The young stem and branches are soft and green, while the older ones have a thin, brownish bark. The leaves, which are shaped like those of the common ivy, are bright green and shiny, and always appear to have been freshly polished.

The head-shaped inflorescences are carried in dense, tennis ball–sized clusters. They are sparkling yellow and have conspicuous ray florets.

The species is indigenous to the eastern seaboard of subtropical southern Africa, but has become naturalized in several mild climate regions around the world. It is particularly abundant along the Mediterranean coast.

Commonly known as the "canary creeper," this is one of the best succulent-leaved creepers to plant in any garden.

Established plants take kindly to hedge trimming and will grow more densely if cut back occasionally.

Although it can survive on very little water, it cannot tolerate subzero temperatures.

×*Senecurio kleiniiformis*

Leaves of ×*Senecurio kleiniiformis* are thin lower down and widen into an arrow head-like blade portion. Inset photo. This form has bright yellow flowers.

×*Senecurio kleiniiformis* is a hybrid between a species of *Curio* and *Senecio tropaeofolius*.

It produces short to elongated, variously leaning stems with widely dispersed leaves along the stems. The leaves of ×*S. kleiniiformis* are thin lower down, elongated, and then widen from a narrow basal portion into an arrow head–like blade. The inflorescences are head-shaped and consist of disk florets only. Multiple inflorescences are usually carried in a branched structure. The small, tightly packed flowers are yellow to yellow infused with white.

Echeveria tolimanensis

CRASSULACEAE

The Crassulaceae is a very large succulent plant family that occurs in both the eastern and western hemispheres. The species of this near-cosmopolitan family invariably have succulent leaves and, occasionally, succulent stems. Most species come from fairly mild climates, especially those that originate in Africa and Mexico. The indigenous European representatives, such as sedums and sempervivums, can easily be grown outdoors, even under northern climatic conditions. All other species need a frost-free environment if they are grown in colder climates.

The flower parts are separate and arranged in multiples of four or five. Although most species are small, low-growing plants with short stems, some attain the dimensions of small trees. Examples include the horticulturally very popular South African *Crassula ovata* and *Crassula arborescens*, and the Mexican *Sedum frutescens*.

In Africa and Madagascar the most handsome species are included in the genera *Crassula*, *Cotyledon*, and *Kalanchoe*. The Mexican and European species that are most often cultivated are included in the genera *Echeveria*, *Petrosedum*, *Sedum*, and *Sempervivum*.

With some notable exceptions, the representatives of the Crassulaceae that are popular in horticulture are grown for their interesting leaf and plant shapes rather than for their blooms, which are often rather small and have muted colors. As indicated above, most *Sedum* and *Sempervivum* species are very hardy, while *Echeveria* will tolerate dry cold, such as found in a cold greenhouse.

Adromischus liebenbergii subsp. orientalis

Leaves of *Adromischus liebenbergii* subsp. *orientalis* are light green and elongated triangular with a rounded apical margin. Inset photo. Flowers are carried in aloe-like inflorescences.

Many species of *Adromischus* have highly mottled leaves that often look like plover eggs. In contrast, the leaves of *A. liebenbergii* subsp. *orientalis* are mostly uniformly light bluish green; the thickly succulent leaves are somewhat triangular with the thin ends attached to the stems.

Flowers have light green tubes and white recurved petal lobes, and, when in bud, are adorned with red tips. The plants are very easy in cultivation and can be propagated from the leaves, which will soon root and develop plantlets from the base.

Cotyledon barbeyi

The branches of *Cotyledon barbeyi* remain erect and carry clusters of tubular red flowers that hang down.

Plants grow as medium-sized shrubs. The stems are thin, smooth, and leafless lower down. Leaf shape and texture vary from smooth and pencil-shaped to hairy, broad, and shield-shaped.

The head-shaped inflorescences consist of a number of tubular red flowers with the petal tips flared open.

This species is indigenous to the southern African savanna. Like most *Cotyledon* species, it is remarkably cold hardy, although its natural distribution range has a fairly mild climate.

Cotyledon barbeyi can be confused with *Cotyledon orbiculata*. However, the flowers of *Cotyledon barbeyi* consistently have a prominent basal swelling.

Cotyledon orbiculata

Cotyledon orbiculata, growing here alongside blue-leaved *Curio crassulifolius*, makes a useful, robust ground cover.

Plants grow as medium-sized, branched, leafy shrubs. The stems, especially of forms with large leaves, are unable to support the upper leafy parts and tend to creep along the ground. The leaves vary in shape and size, from large, bright green and saucer-shaped to oval or pencil-shaped and bright white.

The tubular flowers are borne in small, head-shaped, downward-hanging clusters. They vary from yellow to red, with orange being most common.

Widely distributed in the South African interior, the species grows easily from stem cuttings (the preferred way of propagation). It thrives in full sun, but can tolerate a fair amount of shade. The leaves provide collectors with an array of different shapes and sizes.

Crassula alba var. *alba*

The most commonly grown form of *Crassula alba* var. *alba* has red flowers, here infused with white. Inset photo. Leaves are sometimes strongly red-mottled.

Although the epithet of the species means "white," the flowers can range from bright red through yellowish to white. Leaves are mostly light green and thinly succulent, but the form illustrated here has fantastically colored leaves that are densely mottled with dark reddish to brown spots that become confluent.

Plants have their lance-shaped leaves arranged in basal rosettes that start lengthening when plants approach flowering. Plants can be grown from seed, but some forms will develop sprouts from the base.

Crassula exilis subsp. *cooperi*

Crassula exilis subsp. *cooperi* is a miniature species with its leaves in a rosette. It has pure white flowers.

Even when in flower, plants only reach a height of 2½"–3½" (6–9cm). The rosettes consist of densely clustered, small, lance-shaped, light green leaves that have darker indentations on the surface. The leaf margins are adorned with soft cilia-like hairs. Flowers are snow white and borne in small, rounded inflorescences from late summer to autumn.

In their natural habitat in the interior of South Africa's Eastern Cape, plants often grow in the shade of surrounding shrubs. Propagation is easiest by rooting rosettes removed from a cluster.

Crassula perfoliata var. heterotricha

Leaves of some forms of *Crassula perfoliata* var. *heterotricha* have beautifully reddish purple-colored sections. Flowers are small and white.

These low-growing shrublets have short stems along which sets of lance-shaped, dull green leaves are arranged at regular intervals. The most popular forms of this variety have leaves that have variously reddish purple-infused sections. The leaves taper to a sharp, but harmless tip. Small white flowers are densely arranged in a rounded, head-shaped cluster.

Plants are easy in cultivation but must be provided with a friable, well-drained soil mixture.

Crassula perfoliata var. perfoliata

In times of drought, plants of *Crassula perfoliata* var. *perfoliata* are the only ones that remain green. The dry inflorescences are reddish brown.

Plants grow as small to medium-sized shrubs that often have a somewhat Christmas tree–like shape, given how the leaves become smaller upward as flowering approaches. The dull light green to bluish green leaves are boat-shaped and slant upward and away from the stems.

The small flowers are carried in densely flowered, head-shaped inflorescences. The flowers are bright white with a pink infusion on the inside. Flowers dry reddish brown, making for very attractive plants, even post-flowering.

Plants are easy to propagate from branch cuttings that should be removed from the stem with a sharp knife.

Echeveria nodulosa

The leaves, including the margins, of *Echeveria nodulosa* are reddish purple marked. Inset photo. The flowers of this form are uniformly yellow.

The reddish purple maculation on the leaves of this species is likely the main reason why it has become popular among collectors. In fact, in forms where the marks are a very intense shade of reddish purple, their treatment as cultivars has been suggested, for example as *E. nodulosa* 'Painted Lady.'

In cultivation, plants can reach a height of as much as 10" (25cm), with the lower portion of the stems being devoid of leaves. The upper, leafy parts can be removed with a pair of hand pruners and rooted in a well-draining soil mixture.

Tall inflorescences carry urn-shaped flowers that range from pink to yellow.

Echeveria tolimanensis

The fingerlike, sharp-tipped leaves of *Echeveria tolimanensis* are very fleshy and borne in tight rosettes. Inset photo. Yellowish orange flowers of *E. tolimanensis*.

Plants have small, tightly packed rosettes of almost cylindrical, fingerlike leaves that end in sharp points. The rosettes are carried atop short stems of about 2" (5cm) in length. Leaf color is variable with some forms having fairly dark bluish green leaves; in other instances the leaves are bluish green with a yellow infusion. The upper leaf surfaces especially can have interesting darker patterning.

Light yellowish orange flowers are carried in inflorescences that curve downward. As with many echeverias, the flowers are urn-shaped.

Individual rosettes can be kept in a small container for a long time, but if given free root-run, plants will eventually branch to form multiple rosettes.

Kalanchoe daigremontiana

Kalanchoe daigremontiana growing next to an old specimen of *Portulacaria afra*, the pork bush, in a plant box. Note the plantlets that developed on the leaf margins *of K. daigremontiana*. These will easily root where they are deposited. Inset photo. The color of the pendent flowers varies from dull light pink to a darker shade of pinkish purple.

Plants are almost invariably unbranched and carry oppositely arranged leaves along an erect, herbaceous stem. The leaves are elongated triangules, irregularly folded lengthwise, and at maturity often develop basal "wings" to the blade. These leaf characteristics, as well as the purplish mottling on the lower leaf surface, have given rise to the vernacular names devil's backbone, Mexican hat plant, and alligator plant. When in the juvenile, vegetative phase, and especially when under drought stress, the leaves are short, closely packed, and often variously downcurved. During a substantial part of its life cycle, bulbils develop along the indented leaf margins. Appropriately, *K. daigremontiana* is therefore also known in the vernacular as mother-of-thousands and as maternity plant. The pendent flowers vary from dull light to dark pinkish-purple and are carried on a generally tall inflorescence that is apically branched and many-flowered. Plants are very proliferous in cultivation, can become weedy in gardens, and can be invasive in the wild. Surplus material should therefore be responsibly disposed of.

Kalanchoe ×edwardii 'Fang'

The corolla lobes of *Kalanchoe ×edwardii* 'Fang' are pinkish with hairy margins. Note the tooth-like protuberances on the leaf surfaces.

Most species of *Kalanchoe* are easy in cultivation and will additionally flower regularly in the winter months as they are so-called short-day plants. Where kalanchoes are grown and flower together they often hybridize easily—or can be deliberately crossed—and the resulting offspring is usually interesting and useful additions to cultivate. *Kalanchoe ×edwardii* 'Fang,' with parents *K. beharensis* and *K. tomentosa*, is an example of such a hybrid.

Like both parents, the hybrid is completely hairy and the leaves additionally have interesting, scattered, shark tooth-like protuberances on especially the lower surfaces. Pinkish flowers with frilly-hairy corolla margins are carried in very large, open inflorescences.

Plants are very easy in cultivation and will grow into medium-sized to large shrubs in open ground, but can also be maintained in small pots where they will grow happily for many years.

Kalanchoe longiflora

Kalanchoe longiflora leaves are an unusual sea-green color, tinged with orange. Inset photo. The yellow flowers of *Kalanchoe longiflora* are borne on elongated stalks. The flowers remain erect, unlike those of *Kalanchoe tubiflora*.

Plants are low-growing, soil-hugging, and multibranched. The stems are angled in cross section and quite brittle. The leaves have shallow invaginations along their margins, giving them an interesting appearance.

However, the true beauty of the plant is in its leaf color, which is a striking turquoise blue, softly tinged with golden orange.

The bright yellow flowers, with flared-open tips, are carried on long stalks that can be trimmed off after the plants have flowered in autumn.

Kalanchoe longiflora is native to the eastern seaboard of South Africa. Although it prefers a milder climate, the species is remarkably hardy to cold and drought.

The species can easily be grown from stem cuttings that are established directly in beds.

One of the best uses of *Kalanchoe longiflora* in a garden is as a ground cover. As with many succulent species, the plants remain close to the ground in full sun, but can become etiolated in shady positions. It also grows quite happily in shade, but looks its best in full sun, which strongly brings out the orange tinge in the leaves.

Kalanchoe luciae 'Oricula'

The cultivar of *Kalanchoe luciae* that is known as 'Oricula' has leaves that are incurved along their margins. Inset photo. Close-up of the terminal portion of an inflorescence.

Kalanchoe luciae is one of half a dozen generally large-leaved species of *Kalanchoe* that are indigenous to mild-climate parts of eastern and north-central southern Africa. Plants are very forgiving in cultivation and will easily suffer considerable neglect.

The light bluish green leaves of *K. luciae* are soup plate-sized and often strongly red-infused, especially toward the leaf margins. After two to five years of growth, a plant will develop a large inflorescence that consists of dense clusters of white to whitish green, wax-covered flowers. Plants grow easily from the very fine, almost dust-like seed. Plants can be kept in containers or grown in the open ground.

Kalanchoe luciae 'Oricula,' the cultivar treated here, has leaves that are incurved along the margins. Plants of this cultivar generally remain smaller than typical *K. luciae*.

Pachyphytum oviferum

The fleshy, off-white, egg-shaped leaves of *Pachyphytum oviferum* make it a coveted horticultural attraction. Inset photo. Frontal view of the flowers showing the large, greenish white floral bracts that envelope the flowers.

Plants are low-growing and fat-leaved. The leaves easily become detached from the stem, exposing a short, whitish gray stem with small, but obvious leaf scars. The oval leaves are an interesting off-white color, and resemble small bird eggs.

The nodding inflorescence is quite short and carries a number of small, loosely arranged flowers. The flowers are fairly insignificant in size and color but, rather interestingly, are almost entirely enclosed by large, greenish white floral bracts.

These low-growing plants have very fat, egg-shaped leaves, undoubtedly a feature that makes them desirable to grow as part of a collection.

A leaf that becomes detached from a plant will quickly form roots and grow into a healthy new plant.

This Mexican species is exceptionally easy in cultivation. It grows well in open beds in mild climates, but should be protected from the excessive rainfall and low temperatures found in more severe climates.

Tylecodon paniculatus

A typically fat-trunked specimen of *Tylecodon paniculatus* in leaf. The leaves are shed in winter.

Plants grow as medium-sized to large, fat-trunked specimens that branch higher up to yield a treelike growth form. Stems are generally light yellowish brown with a peeling bark. Leaves are light green and thickly succulent and are boat-shaped to oval in outline. Plants are deciduous, shedding their leaves in winter. Inflorescence stalks are bright red and carry widely scattered, dull yellowish, tubular flowers.

Plants are indigenous to the western, winter rainfall regions of southern Africa. In summer rainfall regions, plants should be protected against too much rain in the warm months.

Portulacaria pygmaea

DIDIEREACEAE

In terms of genera, the family Didiereaceae is best represented on Madagascar, Ile de Rouge, or the Red Island, where four genera have been recorded. Recently, the genera *Portulacaria* and *Ceraria* were reclassified in the Didiereaceae, so that it now also has a representation in neighboring southern Africa. *Portulacaria* has succulent stems and leaves, but unlike the Malagasy representatives, species in this genus lack spines on their stems. *Portulacaria afra*, commonly known as "porkbush" or "elephant's food," grows as a large, shrubby specimen, but can also be kept in a small container for many decades. The stems are pliable and can be trained into a fascinating bonsai tree. It can easily be pruned and manipulated into interesting shapes in the garden, making it a useful architectural plant. In its natural habitat, it is an excellent fodder plant for game, including elephants, as its common name indicates. Some species of the genus *Portulacaria* require protection from excessive amounts of rain. Even if they are kept dry in winter, frost is still sure to induce considerable leaf drop and the tips of the stems will die back.

Alluaudia comosa

The branches of *Alluaudia comosa* carry single spines and egg-shaped leaves.

Unlike representatives of the genus *Portulacaria*, those included in *Alluaudia* have spines that are often densely dispersed along their stems and branches. The treelike *Alluaudia comosa* has a short stem on top of which branches that can reach a height of many feet develop. The stems and branches are adorned with single spines that variously project outward.

The mostly paired, egg-shaped leaves are shed at the onset of the dry season.

Male and female flowers are borne on separate plants. The species occurs naturally in southwestern Madagascar.

Portulacaria afra

Portulacaria afra leaves are densely arranged on the branches and provide the perfect green "canvas" against which a gardener can paint with other species that have contrasting foliage or color. Inset photo. Close-up of the flowers of the rarer, white-flowered form of *Portulacaria afra*.

Plants grow as robust, multibranched, erect shrubs or small trees. The stems are covered with a brownish bark that peels off from time to time, especially after cold spells. The leaves are small, bright green, and thick.

Plants produce clusters of small purplish pink flowers in midsummer. A rarer form has white flowers.

The species is indigenous to the eastern seaboard of southern Africa.

Propagation is through stem cuttings or truncheons that root exceptionally easily. Plants do well in open beds and containers. They can even be planted in small trays and turned into bonsai.

A number of selected forms of *Portulacaria afra* are available in the trade, including forms with leaves that are partly yellow. These grow more slowly than their green counterparts and are perfect for cultivation in hanging baskets. However, the most striking form is arguably the one that sprawls along the ground and over rocks, never rising more than a few inches above the soil surface, making the perfect succulent ground cover.

Portulacaria pygmaea

The short stems of *Portulacaria pygmaea* have a knotted, crooked appearance and bear round to egg-shaped, light green to bluish green leaves.

This small, compact species is for good reason known as the pygmy portulacaria: it remains stunted looking, even in cultivation.

Short, thick, stubby branches arise from a thickened, gnarled-looking, basal stem portion, and the branches are often turned sideways. The light green to bluish green leaves are round to egg-shaped and fat, and look like well-fed ticks. The whitish flowers are quite small and insignificant.

Given the growth form of the species, it is often cultivated in attractive plant containers as a bonsai-ed, fat-stemmed specimen.

The species occurs on the border between South Africa and Namibia. It is sometimes treated as *Ceraria pygmaea*.

Sansevieria bagamoyensis

DRACAENACEAE

This small family of mostly tropical African species is represented in succulent plant collections by species mainly from two genera: *Sansevieria* and *Dracaena*. Species of the former are mostly small, low-growing plants with sharp-tipped, spotted leaves, while the latter are small to large fat-trunked trees. *Sansevieria* is sometimes included in *Dracaena*.

Like representatives of the Agavaceae, the century-plant family, the leaves of many members of the Dracaenaceae are exceptionally fibrous. To this day, people in areas where, for example, *Sansevieria* species occur naturally, harvest the leaves and ingeniously extract and convert the fibers into very strong and durable lengths of rope.

A horticultural benefit of species of the Dracaenaceae is that many of them are very tolerant of shady positions. In their natural habitats they often grow as part of the lower layer of savanna and forest vegetation. This ability to grow well where there are comparatively low levels of light makes them perfectly suited for cultivation in the garden under shady trees.

Most Dracaenaceae species occur naturally in fairly mild, more or less frost-free areas. To cultivate them successfully requires protection against low temperatures, especially in areas that receive rain in winter. In areas that experience high summer humidity, they will flourish under glass, and many species do well when cultivated indoors.

Most species of *Dracaena* are only weakly succulent, the leaf-succulent *Dracaena transvaalensis* being an exception. The most prominent and widely cultivated succulent in the Dracaenaceae is the spectacular, thick-stemmed *Dracaena draco* (Dragon Tree) from the Canary Islands. The family Dracaenaceae is sometimes included in a more inclusive, but rather unwieldy family, the Asparagaceae, an approach not followed here.

Sansevieria bagamoyensis

Sansevieria bagamoyensis has widely spaced, sharp-tipped leaves arranged along an elongated stem.

Plants grow as erect to leaning shrubs that have their leaves widely spaced along a stem that can reach about 3 ft. (1m) in length. The leaves are uniformly light green, lance-shaped, and project away from the stem at an angle of nearly 90 degrees. The leaf margins are adorned with a narrow white edge. The leaf apices are sharply pointed.

A yellow-variegated leaf form is also found in cultivation. The species occurs in Kenya and Tanzania.

Sansevieria hallii

In *Sansevieria hallii*, only a few often recurved leaves are carried in a rosulate cluster.

Plants are clustered and stemless, and each cluster consists of up to three sub-cylindrical leaves. Leaves are spreading and of variable length, with the longest ones reaching a length of just less than 3 ft. (1m). On the lower surface, the leaves are rounded with shallow lengthwise-running grooves, while the upper surface is flat or slightly bulged. Leaves are distinctly or indistinctly crossbanded with lighter and darker zones, and are apically bluntly rounded, but with sharp tips.

Inflorescences are very short and produced at about ground level. Flowers are white, faintly scented, and produced in summer.

Sansevieria hyacinthoides

Sansevieria hyacinthoides is exceptionally hardy, being able to survive very dry spells with no apparent ill effects.

Plants grow as erect, robust, grasslike tufts. The leaves are carried in rather compact rosettes that tend to multiply rapidly, giving rise to impenetrable thickets. Leaf color varies from light green to a nearly metallic blue. The leaves are mottled with lighter green or silvery crossbands that tend to become confluent to form zebra-like stripes, especially in the upper parts of the leaves.

The flowers are creamy white and fairly large, and are carried in a short to medium-length inflorescence.

This species is indigenous to the African savannas where it favors rocky outcrops.

It is commonly known as "rhinoceros grass," and for good reason: with its erect, sturdy leaves reaching a length of nearly 20" (50cm), only a large animal like a rhinoceros would venture into a dense stand.

In cultivation its unique growth form contrasts pleasantly with those of cacti and other succulents.

Sansevieria parva

Sansevieria parva has shiny, dark green leaves that are arranged in a basal rosette. Inset photo. Flowers are dull pink.

Plants have a rather dainty appearance and consist of thin, flat, lance-shaped leaves that are arranged in a floppy, open rosette. Leaves are dark green with scattered, lighter flecks and the surface is shiny. The inflorescences resemble those of aloes, with the tubular flowers arranged around an elongated axis. Flowers are quite long, and are various shades of pink toward the base and whitish upward. In cultivation, plants can be shy to flower.

Plants form long runners that each develop a new rosette at the tip. The species grows exceptionally well in very shady positions.

Sansevieria patens

The rosettes of *Sansevieria patens* have their leaves arranged in a fan shape.

Plants grow as robust, fan-shaped rosette plants that consist of strong, basally closely packed, sharp-tipped leaves. Plants branch below ground level through rhizomes that can be up to 1" (2.5cm) in diameter. The leaves are stiff but variously twisted, making for an interesting leaf arrangement. Leaves are light green and longitudinally adorned with contrasting, darker green lines. The upper part of the leaves is deeply fissured with a lengthwise-running groove. A variegated form of the species has its leaves variously bright yellow-infused. The leaves are often curved, giving rise to the common name "snake plant."

The inflorescence can reach a height about 1¼ ft. (40cm). Flowers are white to creamy white.

Plants do well in the open ground in mild areas, but will also grow very well in a container for many years.

Sansevieria pearsonii

The tough, erect leaves of *Sansevieria pearsonii* are cylindrical and sharp-tipped.

Plants form clusters of erect, cylindrical leaves that taper to a sharp tip. Leaves are very stiff and grow erectly, often in a single plane, giving the plants a fan-like appearance. The leaves are grooved lengthwise and vary in color from nearly yellow to yellowish green, to dull mid-green.

Inflorescences are often quite short but, in some instances, can reach a length of 3 ft. (1m) and arise from near ground level. Flowers are generally creamy white or variously very lightly yellow- or orange-infused.

Given the shape and size of the tough, sharp-tipped leaves, the species is for good reason commonly known as "elephant's toothpick" or as "rhinoceros grass."

Sansevieria trifasciata

Plants grow as medium-sized, erect tufts of leathery, slightly succulent leaves. Small clumps are formed via the production of underground runners. The leaves are a dark green color, with white to silvery blotches, and the leaf margins are often variously colored yellow or creamy yellow.

Because of the ease with which the leaf coloration and size can become aberrant, a profusion of horticultural selections have been named in this species.

The flowers are fairly large, creamy white, and carried on a short stalk. Unfortunately the species is shy to flower in cultivation.

This central African species must qualify as one of the most tolerant of all plants as far as horticultural abuse is concerned. It thrives on neglect but, if given proper treatment (i.e., sufficient light, food, and water), it is a stunning plant with its silvery white or yellow speckled or striped leaves.

Indeed, these plants are not grown so much for their flowers as for their highly decorative leaves, which make them popular as windowsill, indoor, or outdoor bedding plants.

Referring to their sharp-tipped, tongue-shaped leaves, the species has been given the common name "mother-in-law's tongue."

Propagation is very easy through division of the underground runners.

Sansevieria trifasciata 'Laurentii' grows as well indoors as it does outside in open garden beds (above). The leaves of the regular form of *Sansevieria trifasciata* are dark green, mottled with horizontal creamy white sections (left).

Euphorbia neriifolia

EUPHORBIACEAE

At least in terms of the appearance of their expanded plant bodies, the succulent representatives of the spurge, or milkweed, family are the African equivalent of the cactus family. Like cacti, the stems of most *Euphorbia* species are leafless and the stems are often ribbed. However, *Euphorbia* can be easily separated from cacti in that they are laden with a corrosive milky latex and the flowers are actually small inflorescences, called cyathia. Cyathia (singular cyathium) are often yellowish in color; the highly colored "flowers" of the poinsettia (*Euphorbia pulcherrima*) are in fact not flowers at all, but rather leafy bracts that surround the cyathia. Further, the color of the pseudo-flowers of euphorbias are often imparted by the small, but prominent, variously shaped nectar glands that surround the male and female flowers in the cyathia. With over 2,000 species, the genus *Euphorbia* is one of the largest genera of flowering plants. Like cacti, *Euphorbia* plants are mostly also spiny, but their thorns have a different origin from the spines of cacti; for example, they do not arise from areoles.

Milkweeds are widely distributed and occur almost the world over, but the desirable succulent species are mostly confined to Africa and the island of Madagascar.

Some species have both male and female reproductive organs in their flowers, while others are either male or female, implying that at least two plants are required to produce seed.

If grown in colder climates, most *Euphorbia* species need a frost-free environment, preferably in a greenhouse, although those originating from East Africa and Madagascar need a reasonably high minimum temperature in order to thrive. With the exception of *Euphorbia myrsinites*, all the species of the family Euphorbiaceae discussed here occur in temperate regions where they are not exposed to severely cold, wet conditions for any length of time. Most species will survive winters in an unheated greenhouse but some, like *Euphorbia trigona*, prefer temperatures of 41°F (5°C) or above.

Euphorbia antisyphilitica

Euphorbia antisyphilitica is a shrubby species with its pencil-shaped stems carried erectly. Inset photo. The small, flower-like inflorescences of *Euphorbia antisyphilitica* are whitish with a pinkish red infusion.

This is a shrubby species with its thin, narrow, pencil-like branches being carried erectly from a fleshy rootstock. The branches are usually leafless, dull light green, and covered by a waxy substance that limits water loss. The flower-like cyathia (inflorescences) are carried in clusters toward the branch tips, or at the upper nodes on the stems. They have a white to pinkish color.

The specific epithet *antisyphilitica* refers to its traditional use in treating sexually transmitted infections. The species grows naturally in parts of Texas and New Mexico in the USA, as well as in Chihuahua, Coahuila, Hidalgo, and Querétaro in Mexico. It is the only pencil-stemmed euphorbia known in North America.

Euphorbia caerulescens

Like many species of *Euphorbia*, *E. caerulescens* has a cactus-like growth form.

Plants consist of several erect branches that arise from ground level. Stems and branches are divided into knotty-looking segments that are stacked one on the other. The dull green to bluish green stems are leafless and distinctly angled, with the margins of the angles carrying short, sharp, paired spines.

The inflorescences, which resemble small flowers, are bright yellow. Fruit is bright reddish brown.

Even though it occurs naturally in a very arid part of southeastern South Africa, the species is very easy in cultivation and will benefit from regular irrigation.

Euphorbia capuronii

The leaves of *Euphorbia capuronii* are lance-shaped and the flower-like inflorescences are carried in clusters at the tips of long stalks.

Plants are shrubby and can reach a height of about 3 ft. (1m). Branches are about ⅜" (1cm) in diameter and develop from near ground level, but they also divide higher up. The leaves are lance-shaped and clustered toward the upper parts of the branches. The new growth at the tips of the branches is often reddish brown. Spines of up to ¾" (2cm) long are carried on the branches.

Yellowish green to green petal-like "leaves" envelope the small, flower-like inflorescences. The nectar glands are bright yellow.

The species occurs naturally in southwestern Madagascar.

Euphorbia meloformis

Euphorbia meloformis, a low-growing milkweed, resembles a globular cactus.

These globular cactus "look-alike" plants generally grow as low, ground-hugging domes in the shape of a bishop's cap (mitre). Older specimens tend to be more columnar in shape. The plant bodies are angled and usually a dusty, light green. The stems are crossbanded with light brown horizontal stripes.

The flowers, borne separately on male and female plants, are small and insignificant. When the fruits split open, the seeds are ejected with some force.

Euphorbia meloformis originates from the Eastern Cape of South Africa.

The plants are most often solitary and, to the uninitiated, look very much like small cacti.

Euphorbia milii var. milii

The bright red flowers carried on the tangled mass of stems of *Euphorbia milii* var. *milii* will brighten up any garden.

Plants grow as dense, multibranched shrubs. The branches are fairly thin and pliable and will quickly grow into a tangled mass. The entire lengths of the stems are armed with sharp thorns. The light green leaves are club-shaped to oval in outline and non-succulent. They remain on the plants for longer than those of most euphorbias, but are eventually shed to leave the stems leafless, as would be expected of the succulent members of this genus.

The flowers vary from bright red through pale pink and orange to yellow.

This Malagasy species has two claims to fame: firstly, it grows quickly and will rapidly cover a denuded area, and secondly, it flowers very readily.

And, when it flowers, it is a truly spectacular plant to have in a garden. Selected miniaturized forms have been bred and make exquisite subjects for growing as container plants.

It is easy to establish plants from cuttings that grow rapidly and will flower within the year. Plants are frost tender, so some protection should be given in areas where temperatures fall below zero in winter.

Euphorbia myrsinites

Dense clusters of yellow bracts are produced around the cyathia near the stem tips of *Euphorbia myrsinites*.

Plants are low-growing to creeping shrubs that could also form a useful ground cover. The stems are fairly thin and heavy with sharply tipped leaves. For this reason the stems are hardly able to remain erect. The leaves are a distinct blue-green color and only slightly succulent.

The floral bracts are bright yellow and produced in dense clusters near the stem tips.

A native of southern and eastern Europe, *Euphorbia myrsinites* is unfortunately not easy to grow from cuttings. It is very hardy and will easily survive cold winters.

The bluish leaves make this species a very useful addition to any garden. Note, though, that *Euphorbia myrsinites* can escape from cultivation and it has become a noxious weed in some areas in the USA. It can even be grown in a hanging basket, with the stems dangling over the edge of the suspended container.

Euphorbia neriifolia

Unlike many *Euphorbia* species, the large leaves of *E. neriifolia* remain on the plants, including when they are in flower. Inset photo. Close-up of inflorescences.

Plants grow as many-branched, robust shrubs or as small trees with leafy canopies. The stems are light green when young, in time turning light gray. The angled margins along the length of the stems and branches carry small clusters of short, variously directed spines. Leaves are oval in outline, light green, carried in whorls toward the branch tips, and remain on the plants for a long time.

The small inflorescences have conspicuous, red rims.

The species is indigenous to the southern, central, and eastern regions of India and also occurs naturally in some surrounding countries.

Euphorbia nesemannii

A specimen of *Euphorbia nesemannii* that shows abnormal, fasciated growth (branches in the center). At times of drought the stems can take on a purplish green color, as here.

Plants grow as several, fairly densely clustered, erect to slightly outward-leaning branches that can reach a height of just less than 1½ ft. (45cm), but usually remain shorter. The branches arise from a very short main stem. The branches are ribbed and deeply furrowed lengthwise, especially when plants are under drought stress. Solitary spines are borne along the rib margins.

The small inflorescences are carried on short peduncles that are concentrated toward the branch tips.

The species occurs naturally in arid parts of the Western Cape province of South Africa.

Euphorbia resinifera

Plants of *Euphorbia resinifera* have a cactus-like appearance and consist of numerous, erect, densely packed branches that are variously lighter and darker crossbanded.

Plants are mound- to cushion-shaped, robust shrubs that can reach a diameter of 6 ft. (2m) and consist of a multitude of densely arranged stems. The four-angled stems are borne erectly, and carry regularly spaced, short, sharp spines along the angle margins. Darker and lighter green sections alternate along the length of the branches, which end in more or less rounded tips. The new growth at the tips of the branches is reddish brown.

The small, flower-like inflorescences are bright yellow.

The species is indigenous to the Atlas Mountains in Morocco. In its dried form the milky latex is called "euphorbium" and has been used medicinally since antiquity.

Euphorbia stellispina

Euphorbia stellispina spines are arranged in a star-shaped fashion. The yellow cyathia are carried near the stem tips.

Plants grow as small to medium-sized shrublets, with columnar, ribbed plant bodies not unlike those of many species of cactus. The stems can reach a height of 20" (50cm) and are adorned with spines that terminate in sharp, variously forked tips giving the spines a characteristic starlike appearance. The small cyathia are produced near the tips of the stems.

These delightful plants are native to the arid Groot Karoo and adjacent karroid areas of South Africa.

These plants are not as easy in cultivation as one might hope, given their beauty. Care should be taken that they are not overwatered, and the soil mixture must be well drained. Plants can withstand very low temperatures; well below 32°F (0°C).

Euphorbia tirucalli

'Sticks-of-Fire' (*Euphorbia tirucalli*) stems have bright red tips, a feature that intensifies in times of drought or cold.

Plants grow as medium-sized to very large trees. The trunks are smooth and dull green, turning gray as the plants age. The trees are completely leafless, but the green, pencil-shaped twigs have taken over the role of leaves.

Plants are either male or female and produce small, insignificant inflorescences in spring.

This is another spectacular African succulent tree. Its main benefit is that it is leafless and, apart from dropping a few dried branchlets, produces no litter.

Truncheons planted directly into the ground, where a tree is required, will quickly take root, producing a dense crown of pencil-shaped branchlets.

A beautiful selected form, 'Sticks-of-Fire,' has branchlets that turn bright red when kept fairly dry, or when exposed to bright sunlight.

Euphorbia trigona

Euphorbia trigona is almost invariably densely branched, with the branch surfaces beautifully adorned with greenish white skeleton markings.

Plants grow as medium-sized shrubs to small trees that can reach a height of over 5 ft. (1.5m). The main stem is usually very short but carries a multitude of, most often three-angled, erect branches, giving considerable bulk to the specimens.

The branch margins are scalloped and carry short, sharp spines on the protuberances. The surface of the branches between the lengthwise-running ribs is adorned with greenish white, skeleton-like patterning. Leaves are more or less oval in outline and remain on the plants for longer than in most euphorbias. An attractive form of *Euphorbia trigona* has strongly purple-infused stems and leaves.

This species is very popular in indoor gardening and does remarkably well even under low-light conditions. It is not known from where the species originated. It has also been speculated that it is of hybrid origin.

Euphorbia woodii

Euphorbia woodii belongs to the group of finger-euphorbias, so called because the short branches radiate outward.

Plants are low-growing, bright green shrublets, with a strong, central stem portion that merges with the underground, rootlike part. The fingerlike branches radiate from the stem. The central growth point of the stem has surface protuberances and is rough to the touch.

The tiny flowers, borne in small inflorescences, are bright yellow.

This species grows easily in mild and subtropical regions, unlike many of its relatives. A native of the eastern seaboard of South Africa, it is usually propagated from seed.

Most finger-euphorbias occur naturally in rather arid areas, *Euphorbia woodii* being a notable exception.

Jatropha podagrica

Jatropha podagrica flowers are brilliant red, which contrasts sharply with the large, deeply lobed, bright green leaves.

Plants grow as small to medium-sized bottle-trunked specimens. In young plants, the stems are often covered with a light gray to brownish, peeling bark, while the stems of older plants tend to be smooth. Even as young plants the stems mostly have a pronounced basal swelling, becoming thinner upward.

The bright green leaves have deep marginal invaginations and are quite large for such a small plant.

The flower petals are a deep scarlet red which, along with the stem architecture, have made these plants very popular in cultivation.

This species hails from tropical Central America and does well in cultivation in similar climates. Plants are very easy to grow from seed and will become established as garden escapees where the climate is conducive for them to flourish.

Jatropha podagrica cannot tolerate low temperatures at all: a good specimen can be turned to a soft, rotting mass by just one night of frost.

Pedilanthus tithymaloides subsp. *smallii*

Pedilanthus tithymaloides subsp. *smallii* here clearly shows the zigzag shape of the branches.

Plants grow as small, more or less erect shrubs consisting of thin, green branches with grayish-white blotches. The branches tend to branch in a zigzag fashion. The leaves are slightly fleshy and tend to be persistent in tropical and subtropical areas. In more severe climates the leaves are shed when the plants are in flower.

The flowers are small, bright red, and shaped like very small cones that resemble tiny red hummingbirds.

New plants can easily be established from soft or hard wood cuttings that should be placed in a well-drained soil mixture which is kept damp. Given its preference for more tropical climates, it cannot tolerate cold, wet conditions, and easily succumbs to rot.

This is a good member of the milkweed family to grow in mild climates, as it is a native of Mexico and the northern parts of South America. Plants grow quickly and can be trimmed into a nice hedge.

Peperomia ferreyrae

PIPERACEAE

One thing is certain: the succulent representatives of the Piperaceae (peppers and peperomias) are not grown for their big, brightly colored flowers, which are minute and arranged in short, toothpick-like inflorescences. Instead, their fascination is much more centered on their interesting leaf morphologies. Most species of Piperaceae originate from tropical or subtropical areas, making them suitable for cultivation indoors or in heated greenhouses.

Peperomia are rock-loving and grow with their roots clinging to near-vertical rock faces where precipitation drains away rapidly. Alternatively, plants will take root in the small pockets of soil and decaying leaf litter that accumulate in rock cracks. Most peperomias are shade-loving, and often grow in dry sites in forests. Given their preference for shady locations, peperomias are often sold in nurseries as indoor plants.

Peperomia dolabriformis

The leaves of *Peperomia dolabriformis*, commonly known as the "prayer peperomia," have an interesting folded appearance. Inset photo. A *Peperomia dolabriformis* inflorescence carrying tiny flowers. This species is not grown for its colorful flowers.

In cultivation, plants are small, low growing, and soil hugging, but in their natural habitat they can reach a height of 20" (50cm). The species originates in northern Peru.

The stems are very short and brittle, and the light green leaves are the shape of a pizza folded in half. Along the rounded margin, the leaves have a prominent, translucent window.

The flowers are minute, and only visible as little black dots arranged on a toothpick-like inflorescence.

Plants grow quite easily, but do best in dappled shady positions. They prefer ample water and a well-drained soil mixture rich in organic matter.

Peperomia ferreyrae

Leaves of *Peperomia ferreyrae* are elongated bean-shaped and appear to project outward from the stem and growing tip. Inset photo. The inflorescences of *Peperomia ferreyrae* carry tiny flowers densely packed on the side branches.

The main attraction of *Peperomia ferreyrae*, which originates from Peru, is the thick, elongated bean pod–shaped, light green leaves that are carried densely or sparsely along the short, brittle stems.

The leaves have a prominent translucent window along their curved length. The thin, wiry inflorescences are multibranched and carry many, very small, dot-like flowers that are best observed with a hand lens or microscope.

Like virtually all succulent-leaved peperomias, plants remain small-growing and do well when cultivated in small pots. *Peperomia ferreyrae* is best kept as an indoor plant, an indication that it originates from a mild-climate region and does best when grown in filtered sunlight.

Portulaca Pazazz

PORTULACACEAE

The Portulacaceae, the Purslane family, used to be a very diverse group, but its classification was recently refined. As one example of this refinement, the well-known African Pork Bush species (in the genus *Portulacaria*) are now grouped in the family Didieriaceae. The redefined Portulacaceae now includes only one genus, *Portulaca*. By far the best-known succulent that is included in the Portulacaceae is *Portulaca oleracea*, commonly known as "purslane." This is a troublesome weed in many parts of the world and, with its succulent leaves and stems, quite hardy. In addition, parts of the stem will root where they are dropped and in established plants the strong taproot is difficult to dislodge once plants have matured. The leaves and young shoots are edible, though, and often boiled as a vegetable or eaten fresh in a salad. It is therefore a very useful succulent, but since it can easily escape from cultivation through copious seed production, it is best planted in pots rather than in garden beds. *Portulaca oleracea*, and several other portulacaceous species, have succulent, coin-shaped leaves. In other species, the leaves are very much reduced, while some have distinctly succulent stems or roots. The various very showy cultivars of *Portulaca grandiflora* are generally annuals and avoid the unfavorable winter season as dormant seed. They are very popular bedding plants in domestic and public gardens where they provide fantastic floral displays.

Portulaca grandiflora

Portulaca grandiflora flowers come in a range of colors that will brighten up any garden in summer.

Plants are low-growing, soil-hugging leaf succulents. The stems are very short, soft, and brittle. The small leaves are cylindrical and a bright green color.

The flowers are borne singly and are quite large, up to 1½" (4cm) across, for such small plants. Color ranges from deep pink to bright purple. Some selections have double flowers while others have multicolored flowers.

The South American *Portulaca grandiflora* is predominantly annual and has to be sowed every year to ensure a crop of color in a garden. Seed, which is sold in packets in garden shops, germinates easily. A vast range of flower colors has been selected from the pure species with its purplish pink flowers.

It is difficult to beat the wonderful floral display that can be obtained from a dense planting of portulacas. Plants require little aftercare and will happily grow in full sun, and flower where the seed germinates.

Portulaca oleracea

Known as the "common purslane," this variable species usually remains flat growing to soil hugging, but will sometimes develop into slightly erect shrublets. Plants are annual herbs with reddish, spreading stems. The fresh or cooked young shoots and succulent leaves are edible and nutritious. Today it is a weed established in most parts of the subtropics and tropic regions of the world. It was likely introduced to the rest of world from Europe, as it was widely grown by early seafarers as a source of vitamin C. The alternating leaves carried along the stems are more or less coin shaped, but narrow toward the base. The yellow flowers are quite small and not long-lasting. Fruit is a capsule that opens to release the small, black seeds.

Portulacaria oleracea is very hardy and will grow in any soil, even pure sand.

Portulaca umbraticola

Plants grow as small, prostrate to slightly erect shrublets that reach a height of no more than about 1 ft. (30cm). The tendency of the plants to remain creeping makes them perfectly suitable to be cultivated in hanging baskets. The stems are soft and brittle, and a light green color that can be lightly or strongly reddish-infused.

Plants are perennial, but in cultivation tend to have weaker floral displays after the first substantial flowering season. It might therefore be desirable to replenish potted material from time to time.

Selections of the species and hybrids of which it is one parent are very popular in domestic horticulture, with such material often being sold under the moniker *Portulaca* Pazazz. Several different colorful flower variants are available.

Portulaca Pazazz 'Salmon Glow.'

Portulaca Pazazz 'Jumbo White.'

Portulaca Pazazz 'Vivid Yellow.'

INDEX

Note: Page numbers in *italics* indicate projects.

ABOUT THE AUTHORS

Gideon F. Smith

Prof. Dr. Gideon F. Smith is a past president of the International Organization for Succulent Plant Study, and has held numerous positions on the steering committees of international botanical initiatives, including the Species Plantarum World Flora Project, the Global Plants Initiative, the International Association for Plant Taxonomy, and the World Flora Online project.

He has also held positions as chief director for research, chief financial officer, and chief executive officer at the South African National Biodiversity Institute, as well as the John Acocks chair in Plant Sciences at the University of Pretoria. He is South Africa's most prolific author on succulent plants and has authored and co-authored over 1,000 scientific and popular papers, as well as over 50 books, many on cacti and succulents.

Gideon has received more than 15 medals and awards in recognition of his research achievements and environmental leadership work. He is an Honorary Professor at the Nelson Mandela University, South Africa.

Jessica Surface

Jessica Surface is an artist specializing in unique succulent arrangements and living art works. She is the founder of Arosezen, an online succulent and driftwood decor shop that showcases locally sourced materials in handcrafted arrangements and gifts. She leads creative succulent workshops in person and online to share her passion with others. In addition to crafting, she leads yoga and meditation programs for corporations and wellness centers. In her spare time, she enjoys trips to the beach with her two girls and walks in nature to inspire her creativity. She resides in the sunny succulent haven of Los Angeles with her family. She can be found on Instagram @arosezen and @jessica.surface.